A spouse who loses their wife or husband is called a wido
widow. A child who loses their parents is called an orphan
is no English word for a parent who loses their child, and p
that is appropriate, for no one word is big enough to ho
pain. My friends Ed and Lisa Young have sadly joined th
of this club that no one wants to join, and they have s
written down the lessons they have learned, holding on
along the way. These tear-stained pages will help you fi
way through whatever pain you face on this side of heav

Levi Lusko, author; lead pastor, Fresh Lif

With compassion and insight, *A Path through Pain* remind
our darkest moments can yield the most powerful worsl

Chris Tomlin, Grammy Award–winr

Ed and Lisa have written a masterpiece on overcoming tl
of life.

Jentezen Franklin, senior pastor, Fr
New York Times bestsell

In *A Path through Pain*, Ed and Lisa Young share tl
vulnerable moments, offering a powerful testame
strength found in faith. Their unwavering commitmer
as their guide during life's most challenging momen
inspiring and enlightening. Their practical steps for r
pain and finding hope make this book a valuable re
anyone seeking to overcome hardships with a deepene
purpose and connection to God.

Jimmy Evans, founder and president, X

This volume is not written with some lofty platitudes,
every word has been beaten out on the anvil of the
experience and heartache. Read it . . . and reap!

O. S. Hawkins, chancellor, Southwestern Baptist
Seminary; president emeritus, GuideStone Financi

A
PATH
THROUGH
PAIN

A PATH THROUGH PAIN

How **FAITH DEEPENS** and **JOY GROWS**
through What You Would **NEVER CHOOSE**

ED & LISA YOUNG

ZONDERVAN
BOOKS

ZONDERVAN BOOKS

A Path through Pain
Copyright © 2023 by Ed Young and Lisa Young

Published in Grand Rapids, Michigan, by Zondervan. Zondervan is a registered trademark of HarperCollins Christian Publishing, Inc.

Requests for information should be addressed to customercare@harpercollins.com.

ISBN 978-0-310-36695-9 (audio)

Library of Congress Cataloging-in-Publication Data

Names: Young, Ed, 1961– author. | Young, Lisa, author.
Title: A path through pain : how faith deepens and joy grows through what you would never choose / Ed and Lisa Young.
Description: Grand Rapids : Zondervan, 2023.
Identifiers: LCCN 2023026006 (print) | LCCN 2023026007 (ebook) | ISBN 9780310366935 (hardcover) | ISBN 9780310366942 (ebook)
Subjects: LCSH: Grief—Religious aspects—Christianity. | Bereavement—Religious aspects—Christianity. | Pain—Religious aspects—Christianity. | BISAC: RELIGION / Christian Living / Death, Grief, Bereavement | RELIGION / Christian Living / Spiritual Growth
Classification: LCC BV4905.3 .Y68 2023 (print) | LCC BV4905.3 (ebook) | DDC 248.8/6—dc23/eng/20230711
LC record available at https://lccn.loc.gov/2023026006
LC ebook record available at https://lccn.loc.gov/2023026007

Authors are represented by the Fedd Agency, Inc., P.O. Box 341973, Austin, Texas 78734 with respect to the literary work.

Cover design: *Ludyn Juárez and Eric Swanson*
Cover photos: *Bisams / Denis / Adobe Stock*
Interior design: *Denise Froehlich*

Printed in the United States of America

23 24 25 26 27 LBC 5 4 3 2 1

To EJ, Landra, and Laurie and to their incredible spouses, Jessica, Brad, and Sam. You have stood strong in the face of adversity and pain and carried the weight of grief so amazingly.

To our siblings, Ben, Cliff, and Laurie. Your love and support during our darkest hours exemplify what family should be. Thank you for your love and constant encouragement.

To Denny and Sueda', Mac and Julie. Your wisdom and simply "being there" for us gives context to genuine friendship in any situation life brings.

To the staff and members of Fellowship Church. You have walked this road with us and have shown us what an "army of prayer warriors" should look like. Thank you for being the church.

To all who are walking through pain of any kind but especially addiction, we dedicate every word of this book to you. Stay the course hand in hand with Jesus.

And finally, to LeeBeth. You are forever in our hearts and minds, and your life will always serve a purpose in sharing Jesus with the world!

Contents

Running toward
the Storm

Have you ever been in a sandstorm? We have. We were in Arizona several years ago and were blasted by one. A sandstorm is a strong wind that carries dust, debris, and, obviously, sand. Although they're not normally life-threatening, they can be surprising, temporarily blinding, breathtaking, and disorienting—all of which is also a pretty accurate description of what it feels like when you're caught in a storm of life.

Chances are, you're in a storm like that right now. Even if you don't show it on the outside, you're stuck in a storm of suffering, struggle, or even shame, unable to see your way out, finding it nearly impossible to hear the hopeful, encouraging words of God and others. You may be experiencing so much hurt that you aren't sure you'll ever recover. And if you've faced one storm after another, you may have worked so hard just to survive that you don't realize the full extent of the damage you've suffered. You may not even want to know because the very thought of processing your grief and loss feels overwhelming. Your current situation could be the reason you picked up this book, grasping for just an ounce of relief. Or perhaps you realize that what you've been doing to cope with your pain isn't healthy and it's time to make a change.

Maybe you've been through some sort of abuse or neglect. *Pain.* Death. Despondency. Divorce. Depression. *Pain.* Maybe you met someone and thought, "Wow, they're the one." Then—*boom!*—they stopped returning your calls and texts. *Pain.* The rebellious teenager. *Pain.* The diagnosis. *Pain.* Or maybe the deal finally closed or the promotion finally came through and you thought, "Okay, this is going to be the answer to my problems." Then the bottom fell out. *Pain.*

These situations are all forms of acute trauma. So it's understandable that we sometimes find it difficult to get through our pain. It's normal to sometimes feel stuck in anger, blame, confusion, depression, guilt, shame, or bouts of hopelessness when working through this kind of pain. This is especially true if you've been dealing with compounding trauma for most of your life, going all the way back to your family of origin. Your pain may cause you to isolate, to get stuck in feelings of rejection, or to continually seek approval. Perhaps you are frightened of personal criticism, are drawn to unhealthy relationships, or feel guilty about standing up for yourself. You may judge yourself harshly, constantly keep yourself busy, or strive for perfection in everything. All of these can be signs that you are masking deep pain instead of facing it in a healthy way.

The truth is that we're all dealing with pain at some level. If we were to sit down with you for coffee and conversation, it wouldn't take long for us to start talking about pain. That's because pain is a constant companion. If not our own pain, then the pain of someone we know and love.

Don't you wish you could plan for pain? That you could say, "Okay, this October, I'm going to go through a painful patch in life. I'll be prayed up and studied up. I'll have the most encouraging people around me. It may not be awesome, but I'll be prepared, and it won't be so hard." But that's not the way pain works, is it? No. Pain is capricious. It's cavalier. It takes charge. Pain doesn't discriminate. You can't talk your way out of it, buy your way out of it, or even pray your way out of it. In its own way, pain comes with a lifetime guarantee. Pain is the great equalizer—we all have experienced it and will continue to experience it over the course of our lives.

As much as we want to say, "Pain, pain, go away," we have to know that request is impossible. Which means we're left with a singular truth that echoes through the years behind us and before us: As long as we're alive, we will experience varying degrees of pain. And the only way through pain is *through pain*.

Our goal is to help you take the first steps on your path through pain. Because when storms devastate our lives, we may not have control over our circumstances, but we do have control over how we respond to them. And we promise there are things you can do to get through your pain. But to be sure, *through it* is the only way.

We want to give you a language and a voice to speak about your pain and to help you realize that you don't have to walk the path of pain alone. Jesus—a man well-acquainted with this well-worn path—has promised to be your anchor during the storms of life. He hasn't promised to remove pain from your path, but to provide you with the strength you need to endure it, to grow from it, and maybe even to find joy in the middle of it.

On the other side of the storm, you may not be the person you once were. You may walk with a limp, so to speak. But when you choose to process your pain with Jesus and others, you will become someone you could never have imagined—a healed soul. And if you do choose to keep going, know that we are in this with you.

One last thing about storms: When a storm is on the horizon, cows respond by sitting or lying down. Their reaction looks a lot like giving up, leaving them exposed to the elements and out in the storm longer than they have to be. Buffalo, on the other hand, run *toward* the storm, getting them through the rough winds and rains much faster. So right now we are taking our first step together to face the storm head-on as we learn how *God* wants us to handle our pain.

Together, we'll find a path through pain that leads to healing and wholeness.

CHAPTER 1

Pain, Pain, Go Away

As Paul rattled the prison with sounds of praise, so will I praise you in the storms of life!

—Lisa's journal, six weeks
before LeeBeth's passing

If you're a parent, you may have had nightmarish thoughts, the kind where you think, "What would happen if . . . How would I react if . . . my child suddenly died?"

I (Ed) once had these thoughts, and when I did, I quickly tried to get them out of my mind. But one day, that nightmarish reality took place right in my arms. I was home alone with our daughter LeeBeth, who was thirty-four at the time. One moment I was her father, and the next I was her first responder.

What had been a relatively quiet night up to that point erupted into 911 calls, paramedics, haunting red and blue lights, a rush to the hospital, cross-country communication with Lisa, who was out of town, and unending hours of turmoil. When I relive that experience now, it feels like LeeBeth's life hung in the balance for hours. But the truth is, she was probably gone before I had a chance to make the first call for help. The path our family began walking in that moment is one we're still walking today. Lisa and I continue to grieve the sudden death of our daughter. Brutal waves of sadness, anger, guilt, and regret hit us regularly and at the most unexpected moments.

LeeBeth was a bright, intelligent, strong, creative, witty, and faithful young woman. She had unwavering loyalty, a signature loud laugh, endless inside jokes, a brilliant smile, committed friendships, bold words, and a willingness to believe in unproven people. She fought courageously for what was right and had unwavering faith in the goodness of her great God. Her friends and family loved her deeply, and she deeply loved the Lord. From our vantage point, it wasn't supposed to end this way. How did we end up here?

Less than three hours before our daughter's death, Lisa and I had talked to LeeBeth about life. We told her—and we will share later why we said this—"If you continue doing what you're doing, you could die." I asked her, "Do you want to live?" And she said, "Yes, absolutely!" She didn't want to die, but she didn't know how to live with her pain.

In our thirty-plus years of ministry, we've never felt as weak and as vulnerable as we do right now. We have preached the Word of God for decades but have never had to live it out from a place of such desperation. We've had trouble and walked through pain, but not like this. It is only by God's grace that we are doing it.

Jesus said, "Blessed are those who mourn" (Matthew 5:4 NIV). Everybody mourns, and everybody experiences life and death. Death is a part of life. This, though, was an out-of-order death. It wasn't supposed to happen. And that added another messy layer to our grief. We felt lost in uncharted territory and desperate to find a way out.

Navigating the Problem of Pain

Many summers ago, I (Ed) did some hiking in the jungles of Mexico with our son, EJ. We went with a guide who'd grown up in the area. This jungle was full of bodies of water and endless winding trails, and it was dangerous to leave the main path. There was a tree called the *Chechen*, and if you brushed up against it, it would cause a nasty chemical reaction in your skin. There were also crocodiles and an extremely venomous snake called a fer-de-lance, also known as a "two-step snake." This snake is so aggressive that it will basically chase you down, and if it bites you, you have only about two steps before the venom drops you.

We listened carefully to the guide, especially when he told us exactly where to step. He could see dangers we couldn't. He would say, "No, no, don't step there; you could sink all the way up to your chest. You'd be in trouble there." With his guidance, we made our way safely through the jungle.

Now, how ridiculous would it have been if I had said

to him, "You know what, thanks very much. You just stay back. I'll cut my own path. I will determine my own way. I know about the jungle. I've seen a couple of movies. I've watched the Discovery Channel. I know what's happening." EJ and I would never have survived that trip.

This journey Lisa and I are on through pain is no different. There is only one Guide qualified to remove barriers, to show us where to step, to take us by the hand and lead us through the emotional pitfalls, to give us the emotional and physical stamina to keep moving forward—his name is Jesus. Navigating the death of our daughter without our Guide to show us the path, step by step, would have been impossible. But how do we know we can trust God to guide us when he allows such pain to exist?

The problem of pain is perhaps the most profound question many of us raise against Christianity. How could a good God—a loving God—allow so much pain and suffering in the world? All God would have to do is move the geological plates a few inches and we wouldn't have tsunamis or earthquakes. All he would have to do is eradicate the cells that attack our bodies and cause cancer and other horrendous diseases. Why doesn't he do those things? Why doesn't God stop it all? How can we trust God, considering how painful life is? How could our pain have any significance?

These are huge questions—and great questions. They're questions we've both asked God, and I'm sure you have as well. And yet the apostle Paul talks about pain being fundamental in the life of a Christ follower. He wrote, "Since we are his children, we are his heirs. In fact, together with Christ we are heirs of God's glory. But if we are to share his glory, we must also share his suffering. Yet what we suffer now is nothing compared to the glory he will reveal to us later" (Romans 8:17–18 NLT).

As loyal followers of Jesus, we are liberated from the controlling power of sin and death. We are God's children, part of his family, and we wait in expectation of a pain-free forever in heaven with our living Lord! That is our incredible inheritance.

However, the world has not yet been liberated from the controlling power of sin and death. Sin still wreaks havoc in our world, bringing death, decay, and dysfunction—from the smallest cells in our bodies to the leadership of the largest countries. The growing effects of sin lead to evil and suffering that God allows but does not cause.

Paul goes on to explain that pain is woven into the very nature of creation itself: "The creation was subjected to frustration, not by its own choice, but by the will of the one who subjected it, in hope that the creation itself will be liberated from its bondage to decay and brought into the freedom and glory of the children of God" (Romans 8:20–21 NIV).

Wait a minute, wait a minute. *Creation was subjected to frustration by the will of the one who subjected it?* Why does Paul say that? If we go back to the creation story in Genesis, the first book of the Bible, we read that God gave his great gift of life and relationship to Adam and Eve. They lived in perfect harmony with God for a while, but then they rebelled. That's when sin entered the equation, and God allowed frustration to collide with creation. Why? Because he gave us free will. Frustration is the result of sin, a result of our free will, and it ushered in decay and eroded God's perfect creation—a creation that included a world without pain.

The fall of humanity, this rebellion, was not and is not God's responsibility. It's ours. And because of that choice, we live in a place that's frustrated, that is *not* perfect and is often marked by pain. Because of that choice, the storms of life rain on the just and the unjust (Matthew 5:45).

You might say, "Well, I certainly wasn't in the garden of Eden. I didn't rebel against God. Why am I paying for someone else's mistake?" Have you ever sinned? Ever told a lie, even a "little white lie"? Ever coveted what your neighbor had? Ever fudged a bit on some of your tax numbers? Dealt with pride? Battled selfishness? All of us are guilty of sin, so all of us have contributed to the fallenness of the world. But the good news is that Jesus came to pay the penalty for our sin and restore us to a perfect relationship with him! Remember, Paul tells us that our current sufferings are nothing compared to what Jesus can and will do in us. The great hope of healing and transformation is part of what we will be unpacking throughout this book.

Pain is inescapable, yet it is also explainable when we understand that we live in a fallen world. But having that knowledge doesn't necessarily make enduring it any easier, does it? It doesn't stop the hurt, doesn't heal the wounds, and doesn't teach us how to maintain joy and peace despite the constant flow of pain in and out of our lives. Navigating our way through our pain and making progress toward healing is a process—one that requires honesty.

Painfully Honest

The problem with pain isn't just that it hurts but that we have no idea how to handle the hurt. We want to avoid it. Ignore it. Make it go away by any means possible. Above all, we don't want to face our pain—*anything* but that! Why? Because pain makes us uncomfortable, and we're creatures who cherish our comfort. To deal with pain means we must first acknowledge it, and that requires being painfully honest about it.

As part of Lisa's and my decision to be honest about what we've been through, we recently did a pain audit of the years we've been married. Some people a lot smarter than us conducted a study and put together a list of especially stressful experiences that often lead to divorce. When we read their synopsis together, we just looked at each other, not sure whether to laugh or cry. Here are some of the painful events we checked off the list:

Moving. Early in our marriage, we moved from Houston to Dallas to start a church together, leaving behind all our family and friends.

Infertility. Lisa suffered a miscarriage, and we battled secondary infertility after the birth of our oldest child, LeeBeth.

A child with special needs. As a baby, our son, EJ,

was diagnosed with neurofibromatosis, a genetic
disorder that carries many frightening worst-case
scenarios.

The birth of multiples. We had our twin girls, Landra
and Laurie, in 1994 as our church was growing at a
tremendous rate.

A child with an eating disorder. Landra has shared
publicly about her years-long struggle with an
eating disorder.

An empty nest. In 2012, Landra and Laurie, the
youngest of our four children, graduated from high
school and left home.

A child with an addiction. LeeBeth suffered from
alcoholism, and we struggled alongside her
as we did everything we could to support and
stabilize her.

The death of a child. On January 19, 2021, we suddenly
and tragically lost LeeBeth.

As we look back on our life together, do we still have
questions? Oh yeah. Are some of these experiences still
painful to talk about? Incredibly so. Are there times we
are both still angry, wondering why God has allowed us so
much pain? Absolutely. But we also know it is essential to
be honest about our pain, not only with ourselves but also
with God. Our honest anger doesn't frighten him, and our
difficult questions don't intimidate him. How do we know?
Just read some of the psalms, such as this one, in which
David pours out his heart to God:

My God, my God, why have you forsaken me?
Why are you so far from saving me,
so far from my cries of anguish?
My God, I cry out by day, but you do not answer,
by night, but I find no rest. (Psalm
22:1–2 NIV)

That's some pretty raw honesty. And we've all been there, haven't we? *God, where are you? Why aren't you answering? Why aren't you acting? Why am I still in pain?*

While it's okay to ask, "God, why? Why?!" there comes a time when we must also ask another question. That's when we move from "Why me?" to "What now?" At some point, we transition from the disappointment and grief that consume us to the hope and healing only Jesus can provide. Our daily decision to navigate through the pain together with God will determine how well our pain management and recovery go.

Pain, Perseverance, and Purpose

You may not realize it, but you have a choice in how you deal with your pain. You do! You, and *only you*, choose the course you will take through your pain. One option is to stay hurt. You can become bitter. You can sink into depression. You can turn your back on God. You can blame yourself and others. You can cry until you are numb, refusing to take a first step. A lot of people choose to stay hurt and get stuck there. Subsequently, their untreated pain causes collateral damage to their family and friends. That's a brutal part of the pain cycle—pain perpetuating more pain—because hurt people hurt people.

That's why we have to wrap our heads around this idea of facing our pain and handling it God's way. Choosing to stay hurt affects not only us but also our family, our friends, our community, and even the world. There's a lot at stake for those who make that choice.

The better option is to walk the path through pain that leads us to the throne of God. It is not a painless path. And in the short term at least, it may be more painful than choosing to remain stuck. But as we navigate this path through pain, we become stronger, wiser, and altogether healthier. Most of all, we see God more clearly.

As we've walked our own path through pain, we have found that God is trustworthy, and we believe you will too. He does not abandon us in our pain. He is with us, sustains us, and comforts us in it. God shows us how to process our pain and helps us discover the significance it can have in our lives as we grow closer to him and more reliant on him. We have learned that God is bigger than our questions. God is bigger than our pain. God is God. God is sovereign. And God isn't wasteful. There is purpose in our pain.

Let us say that again: *There is purpose in our pain.* Consider this statement from the apostle Paul: "We boast in the hope of the glory of God. Not only so, but we also glory in our sufferings, because we know that *suffering produces perseverance*" (Romans 5:2–3 NIV, emphasis added).

Perseverance is all about how we respond to pressure.

Pressure can do damage, like when it builds up in the plumbing and bursts a pipe. But pressure can also make diamonds out of carbon. So when it comes to dealing with pain, the choices we make about how to process it will determine whether we're on the path to becoming a diamond or a pipe about to burst.

Perseverance is staying power and commitment. But often we bail before the breakthrough. We get tired, bored, frustrated. So we quit because the pressure is too much. But Paul has more to say about all this: "We know that suffering produces perseverance; perseverance, character; and character, hope. And hope does not put us to shame, because God's love has been poured out into our hearts through the Holy Spirit, who has been given to us" (Romans 5:3–5 NIV).

Paul makes it clear that our pain doesn't have to be pointless; it can be productive, producing in us perseverance, character, and hope.

The *source* of our pain is our fallenness.

The *course* of our pain can make us bitter or better.

And now the *force* of it, we could say, is that it is purposeful and productive.

That's powerful, isn't it? We don't enjoy our pain. We don't look forward to pain. But we can shift our perspective on pain because pain isn't agony for the sake of agony. There is significance in our suffering—God wants to help us have a proper perspective of our pain so that our pain can be purposeful and productive.

To better understand what this might mean for you, let's do a fill-in-the-blank exercise. Think about the most painful thing you're dealing with right now. It may be something painful you've experienced in the past but the suffering is still very much a part of your present. Read Paul's statement again: "Not only so, but we also glory in our sufferings" (Romans 5:3 NIV). Now replace "our sufferings" with the pain you're going through: "Not only so, but we also glory in _____."

Wow. You can glory even in *that.* You can glory in it—that is, continue to experience great joy—because it's not pointless. Your pain can be purposeful, producing good in you—if you're willing. As much as we might want to say, "Pain, pain, go away. Don't come back another day!" we can't. Trying to escape pain is like playing dodgeball with an NFL quarterback. He's going to nail you every single time. But we don't have to live in fear or under the weight of pain. We don't have to hurt people, letting our pain perpetuate more pain. We don't have to live limited lives because we're walking around with our hearts in a sling. Instead, we can let pain complete its purpose in us. We can become better, not bitter. We can allow pressure to produce diamonds of perseverance, character, and hope in our lives. We can. The choice is ours alone to make, but we don't have to live it out alone. God's love has been poured into our hearts, and he is with us every step of the way.

God Has Overcome the World

LeeBeth kept a journal. This is the last entry she made before she died.

John 16:33
I have told you these things, so that in me you may have (Perfect) peace + confidence. In the WORLD you have tribulation + trials + distress + frustration; BUT be of good cheer (TAKE COURAGE; BE CONFIDENT, CERTAIN, UNDAUNTED)! For I have overcome the WORLD. (I have deprived it of power to harm you + have conquered it for you.)

A Journal Entry
written by LeeBeth

Amid her challenges with addiction, LeeBeth knew where her help came from. And she was confident that despite her trials—despite her immense pain—she served a God who has overcome the world. LeeBeth was right. God *has* overcome the world and everything in it, including its pain. Including your pain.

If we allow ourselves to feel our pain and deal with it, God can heal it. But we must do the work. The plan works if we work it with Jesus, our Guide. Only he can help us navigate our pain.

Take a Step

To help you move forward on the path through pain, each chapter ends with reflection questions and an idea to help you take a next step.

- How do you respond to the idea that our pain can be purposeful and productive? In what ways does it encourage you? In what ways does it challenge you?

- What comes to mind when you consider being honest— with yourself, God, and others—about your pain? Consider any fears or concerns as well as any hopes you may have.

- Set aside twenty to thirty minutes to do a pain audit. Use a sheet of paper or a journal to list the traumas or hardships you've experienced. How have these experiences impacted you and your relationships?

CHAPTER 2

The Club No One Wants to Join

Walking by faith requires trust in God to utilize all situations to strengthen my faith and show others the light of Jesus. God's light shines brightest in the darkest of events on this earth.

—Lisa's journal, seven days
before LeeBeth's passing

The heart is one of the most complex organs in the human body. And, more obviously, one of the most vital. I (Ed) was born with a heart condition called mitral valve prolapse, which I'm going to call MVP from now on because it sounds awesome. That's just a fancy way of saying I had a loose pipe around my heart. The more technical description is that the valve between my heart's upper and lower left chambers never closed properly.

MVP is fairly common. Early on, I was told to see a cardiologist regularly, but was also told it was unlikely I would ever experience any symptoms or problems. So when I made a routine appointment with my cardiologist in 2017, I thought it would be a lot like my previous visits when I'd left with a clean bill of health. But that isn't what happened.

A few days after my appointment, I was standing in the kitchen next to Lisa when my phone rang. When I saw it was my cardiologist, I got a sick, knotted feeling in the pit of my stomach—the one you get when you know the caller has bad news.

"This can't be good," I said, showing her the caller ID. I was right.

"Ed," my cardiologist said, "you need open heart surgery. Sooner rather than later." He went on to explain that I had severe regurgitation, meaning I had a significant backwash of blood in my heart. Because of my MVP, my heart couldn't pump properly; the remaining blood was seeping into my lungs and other areas and could cause irreversible damage.

Me? A heart patient? I didn't believe it. Not because I didn't trust my cardiologist but because I am *that* hardheaded. So I got a second opinion. I called a good friend, Manny, who also happens to be a cardiologist, in Houston. I asked him to look at my test results, and he, too, called me on the phone.

"Ed," Manny said, "you need open heart surgery. Sooner rather than later."

Yup. I was a heart patient, all right. As it turned out, a fairly desperate one.

Manny confirmed my diagnosis and then took it one step further. "Dude, you could *die* from this." When I asked whom he would suggest as a surgeon, Manny said he'd only trust his heart, and particularly his mitral valve, to the hands of two surgeons. One was in Europe, and the other worked in his practice in Houston. Turned out, the Houston doctor he recommended was one of the top three surgeons for this type of procedure. So down to Houston Lisa and I went.

I kept expecting someone to tell me I was being pranked. That it was all some big hoax. A heart patient? Me? I was a regular member at a trendy gym. I had a personal trainer. I ate clean foods. I had even run marathons! And they were calling *me* a heart patient? They had to be talking to the wrong person. But they weren't. They were talking to me.

Believe it or not, I still had more tests to take. "This is it!" I told myself. "This is when they'll realize they've got it all wrong. I'm not actually a heart patient." They did a heart catheterization test, a stress test, a cardiac MRI, and on and on and on. Sure enough, even though I didn't feel it, even though I didn't believe it, every technician and even the master surgeon agreed—I was a heart patient.

I slowly realized I wasn't getting out of this thing. So I did a little research and began asking questions. I learned exactly what open heart surgery involves—which maybe I would have been better off not knowing. The first thing I read was that surgeons crack open your chest to access your heart. Wow! And they don't crack it open with a polite set of pliers, they use a saw! They cut right through your sternum and then spread your ribs. I guess it's the medical field's version of parting the Red Sea.

Then they stop your heart. I can't tell you much more about that because that was all I needed to know about that step. I also learned it takes considerable time to navigate the intricate valves of the human heart, so my surgery would take about five hours.

The day of my operation, the technicians asked me, "Do you want us to lift you and put you on the operating table, or do you want to climb up by yourself?"

I puffed out my chest a bit. *I may be a heart patient, but I can still lift myself onto a table.* I said, "I think I'll climb up myself, thank you."

I walked toward the table, never more aware of how little I had on, with my hospital gown flapping in the back. Maybe to distract myself—from both my nakedness and my nervousness—I started looking at all the machines and tools around me. I reminded myself that I was in good hands. In fact, my surgeon had operated on emperors, kings, and queens! He had just finished surgery on a former president's wife. He was *the man* for this procedure.

I'm happy to report that my surgery was a success. I even walked away with a pretty cool scar on my chest that looks like a zipper. In the heart patient world, there's a term for what I am now a member of: the Zipper Club. It's a real thing! Look it up. There are T-shirts and everything.

Calling it the Zipper Club is an interesting take on the

matter, don't you think? Typically, clubs are something people want to be a part of. Some even pay good money for membership to some of the more exclusive ones. But no one wants to be a member of the Zipper Club. Not really. No one wants to have heart surgery. Just like no one wants to be a heart patient.

We're All Heart Patients

Pain can be terribly isolating. We think, "No one understands. No one has ever hurt like this. Why me?" But pain can also connect us to other people. It may or may not make us feel better in the moment, but realizing that other people are walking the same road we're on can comfort us over time.

I (Lisa) experienced this the night after LeeBeth passed away. It was late and I was lying in bed with Ed. We fell asleep together holding hands like that for days after. It was like holding on for dear life, that gesture. People look at me like I'm crazy when I tell them this, but LeeBeth's passing brought Ed and me closer together—because we chose to let it.

On that first night, my phone rang at about 10:30 p.m. I looked at Ed.

"Should I get it?"

Then I looked at the number. It was familiar, so I answered it. On the other end of the line was a woman named Candice. Candice and her family had attended our church many years before. Her daughter, Becca, had been friends with LeeBeth for many years and had lost her life to her own personal battles.

"I didn't think you'd answer," Candice said through tears.

As we talked, it was like no time had passed at all. No distance. We were now together in a club no one wanted to be in—the club of parents who had lost a child.

Maybe you're not in that club, maybe you are. Maybe you've lost a spouse or have a terminal diagnosis. Maybe you're in the middle of a divorce. Or maybe your pain is less obvious. Maybe you can't even pinpoint its source. Maybe you ache in the darkness, unwilling to admit your pain to anyone. In some cases, you may be unwilling to admit it even to yourself, which might be the most lethal kind of untreated pain. When you live with unacknowledged pain, no one encourages you in your loss or grief because no one knows about it. No one links arms with you in the pain-we-don't-acknowledge club. But we're all in the club of pain because we're all human. That's what makes all of us heart patients.

The Heart Doctor

There are three of you reading this book right now:

- The person you think you are
- The person others think you are
- The person God knows you are

It's the third one that matters most. God knows you better than you know yourself. He knows your heart—your spirit, the seat of yourself, your morality and intellect. The mysterious, spiritual essence of your inner workings.

Our culture talks about the heart all the time. It says things like, "Follow your heart!" and "Listen to your heart." We speak of the heart as our source of "knowing" when we say things like, "In my heart, I feel that . . ." "I just knew in my heart!" "That hurt my heart."

Here's what we'd say, though. As human beings, we don't really know our hearts. Sure, we know our strengths and weaknesses. We know our likes and dislikes. But we don't fully and exhaustively know our hearts—not like God does. Fortunately, the Bible has an outline for the prayer every heart patient needs to pray. It does! It's right in the book of Psalms:

> Search me, God, and know my heart;
>> test me and know my anxious thoughts.
> See if there is any offensive way in me,
>> and lead me in the way everlasting. (Psalm
>> 139:23–24 NIV)

We invite you to pray this prayer, to make a choice similar to the one Ed did when he chose to climb onto the operating table. Ed had *the man* operating on him. You have *God* operating on you. He is the Master Surgeon, and he wants to help you recognize your pain for what it is so you can process it with him.

This is how God reveals the purpose of our pain and leverages it to bring about transformation in our lives. Because we're finite and we think in finite ways, we might not understand the full purpose of what we're going through until we get to heaven. But God is infinite. His ultimate concern is not with our comfort but with the condition of our hearts.

The hard truth is that pain can help us. Instead of an obstacle, it can become a springboard that leads us closer to God. In fact, it's the pain of realizing the chasm between us and God that is necessary for any of us to become a follower of Christ. When we realize that being the god of our life doesn't work, pain leads us to bow the knee and receive Christ, who took on the ultimate pain of the cross for our sins. But for pain to help us, we must first deal with it. The alternative is to remain unaware of how it is influencing us and robbing us of the life we desire. And the time to deal with pain is now, because there is a lot at stake if we don't.

What's at Stake

We've said this already, but much is at stake when we refuse to acknowledge and process our pain. Ed and I are convinced that much of the evil we face in our world today is directly connected to untreated pain. And this isn't just our opinion, it's science.

When we experience deep emotional pain or trauma, the brain's response is to shut down any nonessential functions, reducing our ability to think clearly or logically. The brain becomes overwhelmed and disorganized because it's completely focused on survival, which is very similar to our response to physical pain. The result of such a shutdown is what psychologist Dawn McClelland describes as a "profound imprinted stress response."[1]

Whenever we have a crisis, especially if it is trauma related, psychological maturation stops.[2] Our emotional growth simply ceases until health returns. Some studies have shown that emotional pain can even temporarily decrease our ability to reason by 30 percent and drop our IQ by 25 percent.[3]

We witnessed this up close after our daughter Landra was in rehab for her eating disorder. When she first came home, it was difficult to recognize her—not physically, though she did look healthier, but emotionally. Emotionally, she was like a child. She didn't want a cell phone. She didn't want to drive. Full recovery required a combination of rehab, therapy, and spiritual healing.

Now consider that an estimated 70 percent of adults in the US will experience at least one traumatic event in their lifetime. Of that 70 percent, up to 20 percent will go on to develop post-traumatic stress disorder (PTSD).[4] Millions and millions of people are living out of a stress response that developed because of unhealed pain. People whose brains and hearts are so fogged up by past hurts aren't sure anymore what's a threat and what isn't. They're trapped in emotional immaturity and unable to cope with the demands of life. They don't trust people. They don't trust themselves! And even though some may say otherwise, they don't really trust God.

With millions of us suffering from long-term mental health issues associated with our untreated trauma, is it any wonder we're in so much pain? Is it any wonder we're all heart patients? A great deal is at stake when we choose not to deal with our pain and trauma.

To avoid contributing more pain to the cycle from which we are suffering, we need to face our pain directly, and that requires a plan.

Four Steps on the Path through Pain

Throughout the pages of this book, we'll outline a step-by-step pain management plan. We're confident that if you follow this plan, there is hope for recovery and healing! We know this because it's a plan based on biblical principles.

FOUR STEPS ON THE PATH THROUGH PAIN

1. Admit you cannot process pain on your own.
2. Believe Jesus is your loving Lord and anchor.
3. Choose him daily to lead you by the hand.
4. Discover hope and healing in community.

In different chapters, we'll work through each step one at a time to encourage you and to keep you moving forward on the path through pain. If you're familiar with Alcoholics Anonymous, some of these steps may sound generally familiar to you. That's because Bill W., the founder of Alcoholics Anonymous, derived the Twelve Steps of the AA program from the Word of God. If we follow these four steps in our response to pain, we can persevere. We can overcome as God establishes a path for us through the pain.

A word of gentle caution: please be patient with yourself throughout this journey. These are not quick steps for "fixing yourself," but rather ongoing steps to help you process and heal and to bring hope to your heart as you face pain from the past, in the present, and even in the future. We have also found that these steps aren't necessarily linear. Once you start, you will probably have to go back and rework a step depending on the challenges each day brings. Give yourself grace, and we'll take it one step at a time together on the path through pain, beginning with the first step.

Step 1: Admit You Cannot Process Pain on Your Own

Our discomfort with our pain is deeply connected to our desire for control. We long to decide our destiny on our own terms. But in God's economy, we gain control only when we surrender control to him.

You must admit that you can't heal yourself. Trying to self-manage your pain will never work because you can't change you. Only God has the power, the octane, the juice, the sauce to heal you. He alone can heal perfectionism, a need for control, egotism, approval seeking, unforgiveness, promiscuity, anger, anxiety, deception, criticism, guilt, and much more.

No, we don't have the power to heal ourselves, but we are often determined to try. How? We go to therapy. That'll fix it, right?

Have you seen the social media memes about therapists?

They're pretty funny. For example, one shows a conversation between a client and therapist that goes something like this:

> **Therapist:** *What do we do the next time we're in pain?*
> **Client:** *Add to cart!*
> **Therapist:** *No.*

We certainly don't fault anyone for being in therapy. We ourselves have a Christian therapist we adore. God's work through her has saved us and our marriage from great pain—more than once! But in the world of secular psychology, there's a limit to what they can do. Mostly, they're effective at labeling our pain, but they fall miserably short when it comes to offering a cure. Now, if they're Christian psychologists, that's a whole other mindset. They're operating out of the anchor of Scripture. But let's be real here. Outside of God's prescription, therapy alone can't heal us. Scripture reminds us that only God is powerful enough to do that. God said to his people through Moses, "I am the LORD, the one who heals you" (Exodus 15:26 GNT).

God did not say, "I am one of the ones who heals you." No. He said he is the Lord, the only one who heals you.

Not being able to heal ourselves is a fact we may have to wrestle with, but it is the first and most crucial step—outside of initiating a relationship with Jesus—to begin processing pain in a healthy way.

Here's a simple way to take this step. Wherever you are right now, say this out loud: "I can't heal me." If you're

more. You would go to a dentist and follow their instructions. If they wrote you a prescription, you'd get it filled and take the medication. Why? Because you can't manage that kind of pain on your own.

Our emotional pain is similar. We need to bring our ache to the pain expert, to the Lord who heals us. It's time to pry our pain away from ourselves and bring it to the altar of Christ at any cost.

God's Megaphone

C. S. Lewis famously wrote, "God whispers to us in our pleasures, speaks in our conscience, but shouts in our pain: it is His megaphone to rouse a deaf world."[6] Why does our world need rousing? Why does God need to shout to get our attention? Because we're surrounded by substitutes and distractions. Left to our own devices, we'd probably all settle for counterfeit versions of his best will for our lives.

When a doctor has a patient who is unresponsive to questions or commands, do you know what they do? They use a pain stimulus. If you've watched any medical TV shows, you might have seen the doctors do something called a sternal rub. A sternal rub is basically grinding your knuckles on someone's sternum, which hurts! The intended result is to rouse the patient using pain.

While it may not be much solace to you right now, it's important to understand that God does use pain to rouse us, to wake us up, to draw us closer to him. Don't get this twisted—God doesn't send pain just to rouse us. He redeems pain by making it purposeful. The truth is, pain is proof of life.

The day LeeBeth passed away, I (Lisa) was in South Carolina. I was there visiting my mom and sister when I received the news that LeeBeth had undergone another binge-drinking episode. Ed had gone to her house, picked her up, and taken her back to our house so she could sober up. Ed had fed her and tucked her in to rest when she had some sort of medical emergency and was rushed to the hospital. I was on my way home, trying to get to my baby as fast as I could. But she was already gone. With members of our family surrounding her, LeeBeth's body was removed from life support.

On a bench outside of security in the Columbia airport, I wailed as she entered the gates of heaven. In that public space, in the early morning hours, I lifted my hands in worship. I worshiped through my pain, praising the Father who loves her more than I ever could.

Pain is not the problem. It's simply not. Pain is a byproduct of life in a fallen world. That's why we say the problem is not pain itself, but our response to pain. And in many cases, our lack of response. Pain hurts. It cuts deep. It takes our breath away. The earth shifts beneath us, and we lose our footing. Pain confuses and confounds us. Pain causes us to question God. And all of that is okay—for a season.

But ultimately, we must come to a place in our grieving where we realize that pain doesn't exist for the sake of pain itself. It exists—at least in part—for the sake of *ourselves*. It exists to remind us that we're still here, that we have a God-given assignment before us. Pain can remind us that *we're still alive*. Pain *is* proof of life.

God Can Take It

A family in our church, the Baggot family, experienced great pain when their eighteen-month-old son Lincoln was diagnosed with rhabdomyosarcoma, a rare type of muscle and tissue cancer. Doctors found a large mass on the back of Lincoln's tongue and immediately recommended chemotherapy. However, within just two weeks, the size of the mass doubled, and Lincoln's mouth began to split at the corners. Doctors were perplexed, and surgery to remove the mass became unavoidable. The Baggots were faced with the stark reality that their baby boy, who hadn't yet seen two years of life, faced a high probability of not making it through the surgery.

Lincoln's mom, Shelly, describes her initial reaction: "I had a lot of anger. I told God the night before the surgery that I hated him. I woke up the next morning and told God I didn't mean it. I just hated the feelings—hated the situation."

Have you ever felt that way toward God, like you could almost hate him? There are probably more of us who have felt that way than are willing to admit it. But did you notice how Shelly moved from questioning God to inviting him into her pain?

When Lincoln had his surgery, some of our church family visited the hospital to pray for the Baggots during the procedure. Shelly said that even though she was sending her son into a high-risk surgery, she felt an indescribable and unexplainable peace amid the pain. By the grace of God, Lincoln's tiny body survived the procedure. Then the Baggots received the miracle they and their church family had prayed for. The surgery was 100 percent successful at removing the cancer, and the nodules found in his lungs had miraculously disappeared. Lincoln's doctors later nicknamed him the "miracle baby" because although he had less than a 1 percent chance of survival, he has now been cancer-free for over a year.

Jesus has led and is leading Lincoln's family through their greatest anguish. New to their faith before their son's diagnosis, the Baggots have leaned into God and their church family when many would have run away. And because they chose to put Jesus first, their family and their faith have been strengthened more than they ever thought possible, which will be necessary for the hardships they face on the journey ahead.

In many ways, the Baggot family's fight has just begun. Their precious little boy still has a tracheostomy to assist with his breathing, a feeding tube in his stomach so he can receive nourishment directly, and a compromised immune system that often requires hospitalization, seemingly on every holiday. And his parents have additional challenges—feeling guilty for not giving enough time and attention to their other son and juggling the health of their marriage along with everything else. The list goes on and on. Could waves of frustration and anger hit again? No doubt. But God is big enough to take it and to help them through it. And he will do the same for you if you let him.

To be a person in great pain is to join a club, but not a club you want to be in. And yet it is a club Jesus was in. And we'll never be above joining ranks with him. There's too much at stake to avoid dealing with our pain. But we can make the choice to shift from "Why me?" to "What now?" We can make the choice to bring our wounds to the Master Surgeon.

God invites us to wholeness—wholeness that is not dependent on our circumstances. He calls us to holiness—holiness that is not dependent on whether we feel particularly holy. He offers us a crown of healing—purchased at great cost and freely given. But our healing is wholly contingent on how we respond to our pain.

Will you acknowledge the pain in your life? Whether it's obvious pain, hidden pain, or untreated pain?

Wherever you find yourself, we invite you to make the heart patient's prayer from Psalm 139 your own and pray it earnestly. Ask God to reveal your heart to you, including all your pain. Only then can the Master Surgeon scrub in and get to work on you, his precious heart patient.

Take a Step

FOUR STEPS ON THE PATH THROUGH PAIN

1. *Admit you cannot process pain on your own.*

2. Believe Jesus is your loving Lord and anchor.

3. Choose him daily to lead you by the hand.

4. Discover hope and healing in community.

- How did it feel to pray the heart patient's prayer (Psalm 139:23–24)? What comes to mind when you imagine yourself on God's operating table?

- What might taking step 1 require of you? In other words, what patterns of thought or behavior might you have to surrender?

- Write step 1 on a sticky note and post it where you will see it throughout the day, or make it the wallpaper on your phone or tablet. You might personalize it by writing, "I cannot heal myself" or "I cannot process my pain on my own." For the next twenty-four hours, say it aloud each time you see it, and then ask yourself, "In what ways, if any, am I trying to heal myself in this moment?" After twenty-four hours, write down any thoughts or observations about what you've discovered.

CHAPTER 3

Plastic Bottles Make Bad Anchors

Let the rain come. Let the water rise.
You, God, alone, are my Savior!

—Lisa's journal, seventeen days
before LeeBeth's passing

I (Ed) grew up across the street from a lake. When I was a kid, my parents bought me a little johnboat (or rowboat). It had no motor, so it was just me and the biceps at work on that sucker. The lake was beautiful but also very windy, which was a problem for my little rowboat because it didn't have an anchor. You'd think my parents would have gotten me one, considering their investment in the boat, but they didn't. I was on my own to figure out how to keep my boat from drifting off course.

Fortunately, I was a resourceful kid. I remembered

reading somewhere that you could make an anchor using clothesline and a bleach bottle, and I'd even talked with some people who'd done it. This was long before the days of YouTube, so when I went to make my own anchor, all I had to work from was the spotty memory of a distracted preteen boy. But I gathered the necessary supplies and got to work. I measured some of my mother's clothesline by eyeballing it and comparing it to how deep I thought the lake was. Next, I infiltrated my brother's sandbox and scooped up enough sand to fill the bleach bottle. Then I attached the clothesline to the bottle with several expert-level knots.

I was proud! "This will work," I thought to my adolescent self. "I know exactly what I am doing!" Except that I had no idea what I was doing. I took my plastic anchor onto my little boat and rowed out to the middle of the lake. "I'll just drop in my trusty anchor," I thought, "and I'll be able to stay in the same position and catch some fish." The sand-filled bottle dropped into the water with a soft *splish*, and I readied my fishing pole.

I felt great about my accomplishment for the first hour or so. My little boat stayed steady as the wind blew across the water. But after some time passed, I noticed movement in my position. Then a little more. And a little more. Eventually, to my surprise, my bottle anchor popped up to the surface of the water. I grabbed it in disbelief. Somehow I had misjudged the depth of the lake, and my anchor had never even made it to the bottom. To add insult to injury, I evidently hadn't closed the bottle cap tightly enough, because most of the sand had leaked out.

I had put my hope in a plastic anchor, and it let me down—no pun intended.

Plastic Anchors

The purpose of an anchor is to lodge into the ground below and hold a boat steady in rough winds and waves. Generally speaking, anchors are made of corrosion-resistant metals, and the best anchors are reinforced with electroplating. They're made to last. My plastic anchor? Not so much. But it turns out my plastic anchor does serve a purpose—it's a pretty good metaphor for what happens when we put our hope in anything but Christ to hold us steady in the storms of life.

Anchors are what we attach ourselves to for security; they're our point of reference, our perspective, our context for life. We turn the attention and focus of our hearts to them in times of need. When we're in pain, we look to these anchors—consciously or subconsciously—for comfort, stability, and safety. That means anchors are not short-term fixes. No, these are long-term coping mechanisms we're talking about.

When we're in pain, we might try to anchor our hope to any number of plastic anchors. For example, we might try to keep ourselves steady with money. We think if we can just earn enough and buy enough, maybe that will numb the pain enough to keep us afloat. Or we might anchor our hopes to a spouse or children. If we put all our energy and focus into that relationship, maybe we won't have to focus on ourselves and our own pain.

One of the trending anchors I (Lisa) have noticed recently is using alcohol to cope with the everyday pain of motherhood. And, yes, motherhood is painful. Parenting is painful! But I've watched what is almost like a social media campaign emerge that promotes and normalizes drinking to cope with the stresses of raising children.

Listen, I understand the less glamorous aspects of being a parent. After I had the twins, I felt like a tornado ran through my house daily. I was elbow deep in dirty dishes and dirtier diapers every single day. I also had a two-year-old with a medical diagnosis and a seven-year-old who was ticked about it all. I barely had the time or energy to wash my armpits with any regularity. That is the reality of having young children.

But romanticizing day drinking or counting down the minutes until it's "five o'clock somewhere" is not a worthy anchor. Using alcohol every night to relax is damaging—not only to your body and your mental health but also to your children. Regardless of how well you "handle your liquor," you aren't *you* when you're under the influence. You are chemically altered. And you're delaying the inevitable, because you can't stay tipsy or intoxicated for the next eighteen years. And parenting doesn't get any easier when your children are older. The problems and the pain only become more complex as the stakes get higher.

Alcohol or any form of substance abuse is a plastic anchor that will fail you and your family every time. If using and abusing substances is how you seek comfort and peace, you will certainly wake up one day and find yourself lost at sea.

Another plastic anchor I (Ed) often see is that of a professional status. Some people can't wait to mention their latest promotion or the last big deal they closed. They can't tell you what soccer team their kid plays on, because they rarely make it to a game, but they can recall in detail the last compliment their boss or a client gave. Their job has become the basis of their identity.

And, hey, there's nothing wrong with being a great provider. We're called to provide for our families in whatever capacity we can. But when the title of CEO, CMO, or C-whatever-O becomes our identity? When we're skipping bedtime prayers with our kids to work late or sitting on the phone during dinner to avoid the pain we've created with our absence? That's when we've tossed a plastic anchor overboard. That's when the ship carrying our marriage and our relationship with our kids starts getting roughed up by the wind.

So what about you? Do you have a sense of what your anchor might be? Here's a quick assessment that might help.

- When you get bad news, how do you typically respond?
- When you have a horrible day, what's your go-to coping strategy?
- When you're angry or upset, what do you typically do to calm down?

In answering those questions, what came to mind? If you were to wake up tomorrow morning and that anchor were suddenly gone forever, how would you respond—emotionally, physically, spiritually? How would you cope?

When we are in deep emotional pain, the quality of our anchor matters more than ever. That's when the winds of adversity rage the hardest. That's when the torrents of rain become torment in our hearts. That's when our very lives may be at stake. Because if our anchor doesn't allow us to dig deep and hang on, we will be tossed around without mercy by our circumstances and become lost in our suffering.

Here's a truth we must embrace when it comes to living with pain: If we rely on anything other than God, Jesus, and the Holy Spirit to be our anchor, it will fail us. Anything else is a plastic anchor. It might give us a slice of hope and keep us steady for a season, but sooner or later, we'll drift aimlessly without anything to ground us.

That's when the questions come. "What kind of God would allow this? Why has he abandoned me? Why am I out here in this storm all alone?" While it's okay for blinding pain to bring about questions, it's important to remember that you have a choice about how long you sit in those questions and how you manage your doubt. You can choose what to believe about God, yourself, and the world around you. You can choose whether to question God's goodness or even his existence. And the choices you make matter.

You Have Choices

Tracy and Debbie Barnes could never have imagined they would be parents of a son with Duchenne muscular dystrophy, let alone two sons with the same condition. Duchenne's is an irreversible genetic disease that degenerates every muscle in the body, including muscles such as the heart and diaphragm that are critical for life. When someone has a child with Duchenne's, they are truly full-time caregivers as they await the inevitable. The initial diagnoses were devastating. Every dream Tracy and Debbie had for their sons, from playing catch together to dating and getting married, ended when Roger and Phillip were diagnosed.

The boys were wheelchair-bound from a young age. By the time they were teenagers, they used motorized wheelchairs and required ventilators to assist with breathing. Roger and Phillip needed assistance with everything; they couldn't even scratch their heads on their own. It took Tracy and Debbie two hours every night to get them ready for bed—positioning the beds, the pillows, and the breathing masks so their sons could breathe through the night. They lifted their sons in and out of the bath and bed. The boys were fed with feeding tubes most of their teenage and adult lives. They both received spinal fusion surgeries so they could remain upright when seated. On several occasions, the boys faced life-or-death emergency hospital stays, and Debbie and Tracy learned lifesaving nursing techniques that prolonged their sons' lives time and time again.

Despite their progressive physical decline, both boys were full of life. Roger never lost his adventurous spirit and always wanted to be where any group was gathered, and Phillip was full of creativity and had a charming sense of humor. They both loved the church and loved Jesus, never exhibiting bitterness over their condition.

Miraculously, Roger lived to twenty-seven and Phillip to thirty-four. When Roger died, Debbie looked at his well-kept fingernails, his clean-cut hair, and his well-taken-care-of body and felt proud that they had taken such good care of him. Early on, she made the choice to serve her boys as if she were serving Christ. She chose to trust God and remain loyal to him regardless of the suffering she watched her boys go through. She chose to find her strength in the Lord, as did Tracy.

It wasn't fair, and it was a hard road to travel, but Tracy and Debbie would tell you they decided long ago to stop asking, "Why?" They choose to trust God no matter what. When you keep choosing to trust God, it opens the door to joy. While happiness is fleeting and changes with circumstances, joy is enduring and transcends circumstances. Joy comes from the deep-seated knowledge that God is in control. Joy acknowledges the authority and goodness of God. Joy flows from a choice to trust—one the apostle James challenges us to make: "Consider it pure joy, my brothers and sisters, whenever you face trials of many kinds, because you know that the testing of your faith produces perseverance. Let perseverance finish its work so that you may be mature and complete, not lacking anything" (James 1:2–4 NIV).

Ultimately, Tracy and Debbie passed their steadfast joy on to their sons and the rest of the family. Despite decades of hardship, Roger and Phillip's joy was evident to all.

Debbie and Tracy weren't perfect. They struggled, got tired, got angry, and were emotionally drained at times, as anyone in their position would be. But they kept going. Some days it felt like a crawl, some days like a walk, some days like a plod, but they kept moving forward. They clung to God's promise that he would be with them through every dark night.

The psalmist reminds us that God is ever present:

> If I go up to the heavens, you are there;
>> if I make my bed in the depths, you are there.
> If I rise on the wings of the dawn,
>> if I settle on the far side of the sea,
> even there your hand will guide me,
>> your right hand will hold me fast.
> (Psalm 139:8–10 NIV)

God's life-giving presence was with Tracy and Debbie every step of the way; without it, they would not have made it. Through all the suffering and pain—even the passing of both sons—they trusted Jesus. As they continue to walk through intensely painful moments, they still choose to trust. They have chosen Jesus as their loving Lord and anchor, and if they could speak to you now, they would tell you that doing so is the best decision you could ever make. He is the only way through.

The Anchor of Heaven

The author of Hebrews gives us insight into the only anchor that holds against the strongest and most painful storms of life.

Therefore, we who have fled to him for refuge can have great confidence as we hold to the hope that lies before us. *This hope is a strong and trustworthy anchor for our souls.* It leads us through the curtain into God's inner sanctuary. (Hebrews 6:18–19 NLT, emphasis added)

And what are God's promises to us during pain?

- He will supply our every need (Philippians 4:19).
- He will help us when tempted (1 Corinthians 10:13).
- His grace is sufficient (2 Corinthians 12:9).
- We have victory over death (1 Corinthians 15:57).
- We have forgiveness of sins (Col. 1:14).
- We have eternal life (John 10:27–28).
- All things work together for the good of those who love him (Romans 8:28).

Wow. Those are some incredible promises, right? When we're struggling, they're promises that function as an unbreakable chain of truth to keep us attached to God as our anchor. And there's another promise we can cling to, one given by Jesus himself: "I have told you this so that you will have peace by being united to me. The world will make you suffer. But be brave! I have defeated the world!" (John 16:33 GNT).

"The world will make you suffer." Now, we don't doubt that promise, do we? We don't question it because this world *has* made all of us suffer in some way. But note what Jesus says about how we can have peace amid the suffering—by being united to him, by anchoring ourselves to him. And he promises that we're not left to suffer alone. Right before declaring that he had defeated the world, Jesus said, "I am not alone because the Father is with me" (John 16:32 NLT). The Father was Jesus's anchor, and he is a faithful anchor for us as well.

When the author of Hebrews wrote that our hope in God is a strong and trustworthy anchor for our souls, did you notice what that hope gives us access to? "It leads us through the curtain into God's inner sanctuary" (Hebrews 6:19 NLT). Do you realize what that means? It means our hope takes us into the presence of God in heaven. We don't know about you, but we'll take an anchor in heaven over an anchor on earth every single time! It's essential if we want to take the next step on the path through pain.

Step 2: Believe Jesus Is Your Loving Lord and Anchor

Step 2 of the four steps on the path through pain is to believe in Jesus as your loving Lord and anchor. So here's an important question to ponder: Is Jesus the anchor of your soul? Does pain drag you away from the throne of God, or does your hope tether you to God's inner sanctuary in heaven? If you're not sure, we invite you to read the following section about Jesus's rescue plan, which will show you how to begin a relationship with Jesus.

Like most aspects of the Christian faith, step 2 is not a box we can check off and then go on our merry way. We can't simply flip a switch and change what or who we turn to for comfort, stability, and safety. If we want to experience the benefits of a soul anchored in Christ, the decision needs to be followed by a process, and that process requires practice, discipline, and commitment. It's a lifestyle.

Jesus's Rescue Plan: The Bad News, Worst News, Good News, and Best News

Jesus's rescue plan is the greatest news you will ever hear, but it begins with bad news.

The Bad News: We Are All Drowning

The Bible says, "All have sinned and fall short of the glory of God" (Romans 3:23 NIV). "All" means *all*—you, me, and everyone else in this world. That's some pretty bad news. When we sin, our sins separate us from God. Think of how big and vast the ocean is; our sin has caused an ocean-like chasm between God and us, and we can't bridge it on our own.

The Worst News: We Can't Rescue Ourselves

We are lost at sea with no way to save ourselves. The Bible says, "The wages of sin is death" (Romans 6:23 NIV). The word *wages* in that verse means "payment." In other words, the compensation we earn with our conduct is condemnation. We're lost and sinking. If we got what we deserved, we would be eternally separated from God. The Bible calls that "hell," and that's terrible news. We're all sinners, and there's nothing we can do to rescue ourselves.

The Good News: God Rescued Us

The good news is that God rescued us when he sent Jesus Christ to do what we couldn't do. He bridged the gap between us and God. The punishment we deserve fell on Jesus. Jesus lived a perfect life and paid the punishment and wages of our sins when he died on the cross. Three days later, he rose from the grave, defeating death!

The promise of Scripture is that "the free gift of God is eternal life through Christ Jesus our Lord" (Romans 6:23 NLT). Can you work for a gift? Can you earn a gift? Nope, you just receive it. That's what Christianity is all about. It's a free gift from God, and the choice of whether to receive it is ours.

The Best News: You Can Receive Jesus Now

The best news is you can receive Jesus now. Yes, right now, wherever you are!

The apostle Paul wrote, "If you confess with your mouth the Lord Jesus and believe in your heart that God has raised Him from the dead, you will be saved" (Romans 10:9 NKJV). The word *confess* in this verse means to agree with God. You agree with God that Jesus is Lord and believe in your heart that Christ died on the cross for your sins and rose from the dead. To believe he is Lord means to give your full loyalty and obedience to him. When you do that, the Bible says you will be rescued and saved. That is how you are rescued from sin, adopted into God's family, and receive the free gift of life forever with Christ. Now, that is some *great* news!

Do you know Jesus personally? Is Jesus the loving Lord and anchor of your life? If not, is there any reason why you shouldn't pray right now and give your life to Christ? If you answered yes, what is your reasoning? You're a good person? You go to church? You pray? You're spiritual? At the end of your life, there is only one way you can stand before a holy and righteous God and be ushered into eternity with him in heaven. That way is Jesus. Jesus does not rescue you because *you* are good; he rescues you because *he* is good.

Here is a prayer you can pray right now to give your life to Jesus:

God, I admit to you that I am a sinner and have fallen short of your standard of goodness. I believe you sent your Son, Jesus, to die on the cross for my sins and to rise again. I turn from my sin right now and ask you to come into my life, to forgive me and cleanse me of all my sin. I give you all that I am and

> *all that I will ever be. Thank you for saving
> me!*
>
> If you made that decision, welcome to God's family!
> We celebrate you and thank God for you.

Working Step 2: It's a Lifestyle

If you've ever made a New Year's resolution to get in shape,
then you know what it's like to try to make a lifestyle change.
In January, you say, "I'm going to lose a few pounds. I'm
going to be beach ready by June." You see a commercial
on TV for a fancy exercise bike and buy it because it promises big results with little effort. According to the ad, all you
need to do is ride the bike for twenty minutes a few times a
week and your body will be transformed.

So you ride the bike a few times a week, but by the end
of January you're not seeing the promised results. It turns
out twenty minutes a day a few times a week is not enough.
It's not enough to shed the pounds. It's not enough to get
you where you want to be. Riding the bike is a start, but the
bike alone isn't going to get you the results you want. If you
want your body to change, you'll need to make some other
changes as well.

A similar principle applies when it comes to step 2:
believe in Jesus as your loving Lord and anchor. Step 2 is
about developing intimacy with Jesus, which requires a lifestyle commitment. To be anchored in Jesus, it's not enough

just to attend church once a week; you have to walk with him day in and day out. That's the only way to shift your hope from a plastic anchor to the true anchor.

Developing a step 2 lifestyle requires spending time with God daily. We devote ourselves to prayer and the reading of his Word. We also spend time with his people—serving them, loving them, and sharing our lives and resources with them. This is how we make the switch from a plastic anchor to the true anchor—we become familiar with our Lord and orient our whole lives around drawing closer to him. It's a lifestyle of loyalty and making daily deposits in our relationship by following him faithfully.

One of the daily practices I (Lisa) have used to develop a lifestyle of intimacy with God is writing my thoughts and prayers in a journal. I have many notebooks full of journal entries from over the years. Not all of them are hymns of praise either. I've recorded some tough conversations with God on those pages—especially in the days and weeks after the loss of LeeBeth. There are a lot of pointed questions.

Why us, Lord?
Why her?
Why our family?
Have I not obeyed you?
Could I have done something to prevent this?

Here's one entry I wrote two weeks after LeeBeth's passing:

Oh, Lord, I lean on you as my heart is weary. I stand on your truth, promise, and comfort. These gifts are real, but my heart hurts so much. I remember the healthy LeeBeth and don't understand the underlying struggle. I wonder if I did enough. This haunts me sporadically—I have confidence at most times, but then things come into my mind, and my heart deflates like a slow-leaking balloon. Only you, Lord, can patch my heart back together and forgive me of anything I did wrong. The past can't be changed, but you can teach me through my brokenness. I am but a helpless child. I am nothing without you!

While nothing could have prepared me for the tragic loss of LeeBeth, losing her wasn't compounded by the loss of my anchor. After years of making consistent deposits in my relationship with Jesus—through prayer, Bible study, journaling, worship, serving, and more—my anchor held.

The winds and rains of adversity are in the forecast of everyone's life. And there is no way to remove the sting of pain. None. We are naive to think otherwise. While that's a sobering reality, it can also be an empowering one. Think about it. If you know that bad weather is a certainty, what do you do? You plan for it. You might stock up on nonperishable food, put new batteries in your flashlight, or buy extra candles in case the power goes out. You may not know when a storm will strike, but you have a plan in place so you're prepared when it does. And as strange as it may sound, you can use the same approach for the storms of life. You may not know when pain will strike, but there are some things you can do to prepare for it.

Preparing for Pain

"Oh, she's in a better place."

"At least she isn't suffering anymore."

"You just can't prepare for a loss like this."

Many people said things like this to us when we lost LeeBeth. Everyone meant well and wanted to offer us some comfort, but nothing anyone said could lessen the anguish gripping our souls. However, that third statement about preparing for loss made me (Lisa) stop and think.

In the moment, I'm sure I mumbled some sort of response, but as the fog of initial shock cleared, those words came back to me. And do you know what I realized? They were wrong. While we couldn't predict that our adult daughter would die a sudden and tragic death, we could prepare for it and other unimaginable circumstances in life.

How? By taking hold of the hope found in our anchor, Jesus Christ. We grasp tighter. Day in and day out, we rely on him and him alone. We walk with him. We learn to discern his voice from the deceptive voices of our culture. We grow more familiar with his character. We learn to trust our heavenly Father, who has promised never to leave us or forsake us.

If we know the forecast of life includes storms, the wisest course of action is to gather our emergency supplies and get our rain gear ready. Unfortunately, too many of us aren't prepared when the storm rolls in. "Whoa!" we say, shocked. "I'd better change out of these flip-flops! I'd better grab a raincoat and some boots!" And while we're rushing around at the last minute, our boat is being tossed up and down and thrown off course. But if we prepare for pain, we'll be ready when the storm strikes.

Did you know that the stronger the winds blow, the deeper an anchor sinks into the ground? Something similar happens in a relationship with Jesus. You may have witnessed this when people in your life were dealt some tough blows and still kept going. Perhaps you wondered, "How have they kept the faith through it all?" The answer is that when they faced storms while clinging to their hope found only in Christ, the more their confidence in him deepened. The tighter they held to their hope through the storm, the more secure their thoughts and emotions became, regardless of their circumstances.

Think about your spiritual life right now. How strong and intimate is your relationship with your Father in heaven? Are you praying and studying his Word daily, or is your relationship circumstantial? Is it good on the good days and nonexistent on the challenging ones? It's okay to be angry with God sometimes, but it's not okay to ghost God like you would a bad date. The sign of a healthy relationship isn't the absence of conflict, but a commitment to work through the conflict. The same is true for your relationship with the Lord.

Making daily deposits in your relationship with God is how you make the Lord the anchor of your soul. And there's no better motivation to prepare for pain than knowing your anchor will hold.

The Only Anchor That Gives Hope

If I (Lisa) weren't anchored to my Savior, my boat would have capsized long ago. I would not be standing. Here are just a few of the gale-force winds I've faced.

My mother battled debilitating depression throughout my childhood and was later diagnosed with dementia, which eventually took her life. When we moved to Dallas to start Fellowship Church, it took every bit of Jesus to sustain my marriage and my faith. I suffered a terrible miscarriage and was unsure if I'd ever have more children. Our only son was diagnosed with neurofibromatosis. Our sweet daughter Landra battled an eating disorder. Ed had unexpected open heart surgery. Then our sweet LeeBeth died.

When our family gathered around LeeBeth's hospital bed—with me on FaceTime in an airport—we sang a song together as doctors disconnected the machines that were keeping her fragile body alive.

> How great is our God, and all will see
> How great, how great is our God.

And we meant it.

People hear that part of our story, and they have questions. "How could you sing that? Surely you didn't mean it—at least not at that moment. Surely you couldn't have worshiped the same God who allowed your child to die so suddenly."

I loved my child recklessly, and I still do. I would never have had the strength to sing of God's greatness and mean it had I not been anchored to the gates of heaven itself. As we sang around LeeBeth's bed, Jesus was the only anchor that gave hope to our souls. Anything else would have been nothing more than a plastic anchor filled with sand in the middle of a typhoon. How great is our God for giving our family hope in that dark hour—and we know he wants to do the same for you.

Take a Step

FOUR STEPS ON THE PATH THROUGH PAIN

1. Admit you cannot process pain on your own.

2. *Believe Jesus is your loving Lord and anchor.*

3. Choose him daily to lead you by the hand.

4. Discover hope and healing in community.

- Are you prepared to take step 2 on the path through pain? What patterns of thought and behavior would you have to change to take that step?

- What or whom have you used as a plastic anchor in your own life? What was the result?

- Create a plan to help you consistently lean into Jesus as you process your pain with him. You might add a ten-minute quiet time of reading the Bible or a devotional to your daily routine. Or you could expand your current quiet time to include a few moments of listening to worship music. Now is the time to bolster that relationship through intention and action. Write down your plan. Maybe it's something you commit to for thirty days—maybe for a year! Set a reminder on your phone for accountability.

CHAPTER 4

When Crisis Calls

*My heart seems to be crumbled in
pieces, shattered like a windshield
hit by a rock. . . . Lord, Ed and I
have trusted you with our whole
lives. We trust you with our
parenting. I know I failed. But I
also know that you fill in the gaps.*

—Lisa's first journal entry
after LeeBeth's passing

It was late morning on the day LeeBeth would die that I
(Lisa) received a pocket call from her. It happened just as
I'd arrived at my mom's house in South Carolina. Once I
realized it was an accidental call, I hung up and dialed her
back. There was no answer.

Not long after, I received another call, this time from
Landra. "Mom," she said, "LeeBeth pocket called me.
Something terrible is happening." I knew she was right.

LeeBeth had a history. What started off as a few poor choices in dating had resulted in a reality LeeBeth did not feel like she could emotionally manage on her own. These failed relationships, combined with her desire to be married and have a family, left her devastated. They left our creative, brilliant, and capable daughter desperately grasping for emotional relief from the compounded pain life can bring. If anything, LeeBeth's story teaches us how quickly micro pain can become macro pain. A few poor decisions led to a few worse decisions. Then LeeBeth was self-medicating with alcohol and Adderall, a prescription drug most often used to treat attention deficit hyperactivity disorder (ADHD).

After three episodes of binge-drinking (that we were aware of), the decision was made for LeeBeth to attend a rehabilitation facility in South Texas. She completed the program successfully and returned home. She connected locally with a counselor, and we thought she was doing better. She returned to her job at our church, and by all accounts, she was managing her pain in a healthy way.

But after I learned LeeBeth had also called Landra accidentally, I knew. I just knew. I called Ed—this was his crisis call. "Honey, I don't think LeeBeth is doing well," I said. He went to LeeBeth's house, where he found her passed out on the floor. I won't go into too much detail describing the scene surrounding our firstborn, but suffice it to say, it was every parent's nightmare.

I debated whether I should fly back home immediately,

but eventually made the decision to stay in South Carolina. Ed and I were in constant communication throughout the day. He took LeeBeth to meet with her counselor. He was able to feed her and sober her up some. Then he took her back to our house, where he tucked her in for the night.

That's when I received a call. *The* call. "Lisa," Ed said, "something's happened to LeeBeth. I think she's had a seizure, and she's unresponsive."

When crisis calls, you just know. When something terrible has happened and the phone rings, there's a knock at the door, or an email lands in your inbox, you just *know*.

You receive a middle-of-the-night call, and the voice on the other end of the line says, "It's your mom. They've rushed her to the hospital. It doesn't look good."

You're invited into your supervisor's office, and he informs you that the company is downsizing and your position has been eliminated.

You've been dating a special girl for a year. You thought she was Miss Right, but out of nowhere she texts you to say that she wants to date other people.

Your husband of eighteen years looks at you across the breakfast table and says simply, "I want a divorce." Or your wife informs you, "I'm having an affair."

These are all crisis situations. And just like a storm at sea, they can strike out of nowhere. The winds blow, the rains fall, and giant waves threaten to capsize your boat. You're blindsided and don't know which way to turn or what to do. You're in crisis.

What Would You Do in a Crisis?

When we think about those who have endured an epic storm-like crisis, perhaps the first name that comes to mind is the biblical character Job. Here's how Job's crisis story began:

> One day when Job's sons and daughters were feasting at the oldest brother's house, a messenger arrived at Job's home with this news: "Your oxen were plowing, with the donkeys feeding beside them, when the Sabeans raided us. They stole all the animals and killed all the farmhands. I am the only one who escaped to tell you."
>
> While he was still speaking, another messenger arrived with this news: "The fire of God has fallen from heaven and burned up your sheep and all the shepherds. I am the only one who escaped to tell you."
>
> While he was still speaking, a third messenger arrived with this news: "Three bands of Chaldean raiders have stolen your camels and killed your servants. I am the only one who escaped to tell you."
>
> While he was still speaking, another messenger arrived with this news: "Your sons and daughters were feasting in their oldest brother's home. Suddenly, a powerful wind swept in from the wilderness and hit the house on all sides. The house collapsed, and all your children are dead. I am the only one who escaped to tell you." (Job 1:13–19 NLT)

If any of us had been in Job's shoes, by the time the third

servant entered the room, we would have been on our feet in shock and outrage. "Why, God? Why all of this? And why all at once?" But when the fourth messenger arrived, before he even had a chance to speak, Job knew—he just knew—more pain was coming. When the messenger announced the death of his children—all of them—Job was no doubt brought to his knees in agony. And just when Job seemingly had nothing left to lose, he broke out with painful sores all over his body (Job 2:7). It was so bad that the only thing Job knew to do was to sit in ashes and use some pottery shards to scrape his sores.

We read about Job, and we hear about stories like LeeBeth's, and we think, "What would I do in that situation? How would I handle that crisis?" Maybe you are in a crisis right now and you're asking yourself that very question: "What do I do now?"

Just as there was no how-to manual for Job, no one gives us a handout for navigating the unique challenges we face when our own crisis comes calling. But that doesn't mean we have nothing to go by. God has given us a crisis survival guide in his Word. It's what Ed and I have clung to for dear life!

Stages of Grief and Pain

One of the hardest parts of navigating a crisis is not knowing what might happen next. While we can't tell you what to expect from your circumstances, we can give you some idea of what to expect as you go through the stages of grief and pain. Although you may find yourself bouncing around among these stages rather than moving straight through them, we hope this framework gives you context for what you're going through.

These are the five stages of grief and pain as we have experienced them on our journey. As you read through each of the stages, consider which one(s) you resonate with most right now.

STAGES OF GRIEF AND PAIN

Shock: Denial, disbelief, distraction, and disconnection

Struggle: Anger, blaming (God, ourselves, and others), confusion, depression, emptiness, frustration, guilt, and hopelessness

Surrender: Choosing to find hope and healing in Christ and his community

Sailing: Navigating the waves of grief and pain with Jesus

Sharing: Using your pain and experiences to help and bring hope to others

Your Crisis Survival Guide

I (Ed) recently talked to a family who had just returned from a cruise. They were gone for a week and had a wonderful time. When I asked them to describe the cruise, they said the first thing they did—before they even left port—was an emergency drill. The captain gathered all 2,500 passengers on deck and had them put on their life preservers and locate their life rafts. The captain also pointed out that there was a sign posted on the back of every cabin door that outlined evacuation routes and what to do in case of emergency.

That's when it struck me that the Christian life is kind of like going on a cruise. Jesus invites you and me to climb aboard this beautiful vessel. He says, "I am going to captain your ship. This voyage will be the most exciting adventure you can ever imagine. Come aboard! All expenses paid, and it's for eternity!" And then he adds, "But I'm going to warn you that you will encounter rough seas and storms. Your ship will be rocked. You may sometimes feel like you and your faith are sinking."

And just as the cruise ship captain didn't leave his passengers to guess how to survive in case of emergency, Jesus provides us with a crisis survival guide—the Bible. He tells us if we apply the truths and principles it contains, we will be able to navigate our way through even the most painful storms of life.

But the Bible isn't always the first place we turn to in a crisis. Instead, when crisis calls, we often retreat. We turn inward and shut down. We take shelter in our own little cabin on the ship, slam the door shut, and lock it. "I can handle this alone," we think. Or maybe more honestly, "I don't think I can take this. I don't think I'll make it through this storm. I don't know what else to do, so I'm going to withdraw." And yet what we need most at times like these is to be out of our own heads and immersed in the power and principles of God's Word.

Three Principles to Help You Move from "Why Me?" to "What Now?"

When crisis calls, the first place we should take our pain is to the pages of God's survival guide, written for us. In those pages, we find principles we can stand on that will move us from "Why me?" (shock and struggle) to "What now?" (sailing and sharing). And three of the most important principles to understand are these: God is not your enemy, God is your security, and God desires intimacy with you.

PRINCIPLE 1: GOD IS NOT YOUR ENEMY

We have to realize and accept that while God allows storms to hit your life and mine, he is not the storm maker; Satan is. Satan is the instigator and the mastermind behind all the evil in the world.

We see this clearly in Job's crisis story. The Bible tells us that Satan approached God to trash-talk Job: "You have made him prosper in everything he does. . . . But reach out and take away everything he has, and he will surely curse you to your face!" (Job 1:10–11 NLT). But Satan was wrong. Here's how Job responded when he lost everything:

Job got up and tore his clothes in grief. He shaved his head and threw himself face downward on the ground.

He said, "I was born with nothing, and I will die with nothing. The LORD gave, and now he has taken away. May his name be praised!"

In spite of everything that had happened, Job did not sin by blaming God. (Job 1:20–22 GNT)

Remember, because we've sinned, we live in a fallen world; and because our world is fallen, we will encounter evil and crises. That may be difficult to understand and hard to accept, but to blame God for the storms of life would be inaccurate.

Recognize that Satan is the enemy, and resist the temptation to distance yourself from God out of anger or misplaced blame. You might argue, "But I'm not distancing myself from God. I just don't understand. Why me?" But do you know what you're really saying when you ask, "Why me?" Here's the full expression of that question: "God, why did you make this happen to me? Why did you perpetrate this hurt on me and on my family? God, explain yourself to me."

I (Lisa) was full of questions for God in the wake of LeeBeth's passing. "Why? Why did LeeBeth have to die? Why do other people do much worse and live? Why are we going through this hellacious time when we have served God faithfully? Why couldn't her story be the story of victory here on earth? Why did God cause this to happen? Why, why, why?"

I accepted Christ when I was nine years old, and I have always loved the Lord and tried my best to obey his commands. I have sinned—of course I have—but I have never rebelled. I remember when I first read the book of Job and something akin to a shiver of dread went through me. *I hope the Lord doesn't allow Satan to test me*, is what that shiver said. *I don't want to be like Job.* No one does. No one wants to endure pain or loss or suffering.

Even Job got to the point where he asked, "Why me?" Not long after becoming sick, Job threw himself a pity party. The Bible records a monologue that goes on for many chapters in which Job asked all kinds of *why* questions—why hadn't he died at birth, why did God keep testing him, and why wouldn't God simply allow him to die? And then he said this:

> I am tired of living.
>> Listen to my bitter complaint.
> Don't condemn me, God.
>> Tell me! What is the charge against me?
> Is it right for you to be so cruel?
>> (Job 10:1–3 GNT)

Job asked what many of us ask when pain levels us: "What have I done to deserve this? Why me, God? Why me?" After Job's long lament, God responded to Job in an interesting way. He said,

> Who are you to question my wisdom
>> with your ignorant, empty words?
> Now stand up straight

and answer the questions I ask you.
Were you there when I made the world?
   If you know so much, tell me about it. . . .
Can you shout orders to the clouds
   and make them drench you with rain?
And if you command the lightning to flash,
   will it come to you and say, "At your
      service"? (Job 38:2–4, 34–35 GNT)

God kind of played a game of Not-So-Trivial Pursuit with Job, saying, "Okay, Job, think fast. Category: History. Where were you, Job, when I laid the foundations of the earth? That's right. You weren't there. Next category: Sports and Leisure. Job, have you ever on a Sunday afternoon kind of just played with lightning bolts? No? Didn't think so." And on it went.

The book of Job devotes four whole chapters to God's response (Job 38–41). In his response, God asked Job this killer question: "Are you trying to prove that I am unjust—to put me in the wrong and yourself in the right?" (Job 40:8 GNT).

Wow. Have you ever thought about it that way? That when we ask, "Why me?" we're essentially putting ourselves in the right and God in the wrong?

No, God is not the enemy. And Job finally realized that. He said,

I know, LORD, that you are all-powerful;
   that you can do everything you want.

> You ask how I dare question your wisdom
>> when I am so very ignorant.
> I talked about things I did not understand,
>> about marvels too great for me to know.
>> (Job 42:2–3 GNT)

We have a very real enemy—Satan. He is a liar and a thief. When we're in pain and we need someone to be mad at, *he* is the one to be mad at. The temptation to blame God and ask, "Why me?" is incredibly strong when we're hurting. In our anguish, we may want to distance ourselves or turn away from our Father in heaven. But that will not lead us forward on the path to healing. Instead, we must stay anchored to Christ, connected to heaven by the truth of God's Word, and accept that God is not the enemy.

PRINCIPLE 2: GOD IS YOUR SECURITY

Even when the storm seems fierce and unending, know that God will give you the power and provide the resources to get through it. He will lead you through any hardship when you rely on him. How do we know? It's in his crisis survival guide, the Bible.

A powerful passage in Isaiah repeats one word we can cling to during the storms and pain of life. See if you can pick up on what that word is:

> When you pass through deep waters, I will be
>> with you;
>> your troubles will not overwhelm you.

When you pass through fire, you will not be
    burned;
    the hard trials that come will not hurt you.
For I am the LORD your God,
    the holy God of Israel, who saves you.
        (Isaiah 43:2–3 GNT)

If you noticed the two uses of the word *through*, you got it right. Embedded in the word *through* is a promise—you *will* reach the other side. You will pass through the deep waters and through the fire.

God does not promise immediate escape, but he does promise a way through the trial when you persevere under the pressure and remain loyal to him. He will guide you, protect you, heal you, and help you grow. Though at times your journey through pain may feel like it's one step forward and two steps back, you won't be crushed beneath the weight of your pain and challenges. You won't stall out. You won't succumb to despair. Why? Because you have this blessed promise: "When you pass through deep waters, I will be with you."

I will be with you in the hospital room.
I will be with you at the divorce hearing.
I will be with you at the graveside service.
I will be with you at the rehabilitation facility.
I will be with you when you pack your bags to leave.
I will be with you when you enter that meeting.
I will be with you when you are all alone.

I will be with you.
I will see you through to the other side of it.
I will be with you on the path through pain.

God has promised to see you through your pain, to help you navigate your crisis. When the skies turn black and the winds threaten to capsize your boat, reach out to God as your life preserver. He is your security.

PRINCIPLE 3: GOD DESIRES INTIMACY

Job was a righteous man. He was obedient to God and devoted himself to living with integrity and doing the right things. But until Job was allowed to suffer, he didn't know God intimately. In that sense, we might say Job was spiritually immature—more of a rule follower than a lover of God.

When God confronted Job with that killer question, "Are you trying to prove that I am unjust—to put me in the wrong and yourself in the right?" (Job 40:8 GNT), Job responded with contrition and repentance. He said,

> You told me to listen while you spoke
> and to try to answer your questions.
> In the past I knew only what others had told me,
> but now I have seen you with my own eyes.
> So I am ashamed of all I have said
> and repent in dust and ashes. (Job 42:4–6 GNT)

Job's faith had been based on the stories of others—on

the faith of others. He knew God's laws and obeyed them, but he didn't know God. Until he started walking the path through pain, he hadn't personally experienced the redemption of God. Job's reward for persevering was to see God with his own eyes; and that encounter gave Job a whole new perspective—not only on his suffering but also on who God is.

After Job's repentance, God showed him favor. The last part of Job's life was even more blessed than the first: "The LORD made him prosperous again and gave him twice as much as he had had before" (Job 42:10 GNT). But more than the children and the livestock God restored, Job received life's greatest blessing: intimacy with God. When we're in crisis, Job's story teaches us not to focus on the *why* of our suffering but on the *who*—the God who is with us through it.

God is *not* your enemy. Rather, he's the kryptonite to your enemy—he's your security. But to experience his ever-present help, you must establish intimacy with your heavenly Father. Maybe you need to invite God into the darkness of your pain. Maybe you need to repent like Job did. Maybe you need to do both. I promise that whatever steps you take toward God are also steps you're taking on the path through pain.

The Change That Changed Everything

After a tragic car accident, Lindsey woke up in the ICU with a broken neck and back, among several other injuries.

Doctors said she would never walk again. Now bound to a wheelchair, Lindsey felt hopeless; she knew the road ahead would be extremely difficult. She and her husband, JP, thought they understood what it meant to be Christ followers, but in the middle of their greatest crisis, they realized they had merely been going through the motions. In the weeks after the accident, they learned that faith can't be trusted until it has been tested. Their previous life of simply going to church on the weekends had not prepared them for what they were going through.

When Lindsey and JP realized they had kept God at a distance, they decided to make a change. While she was still in intensive physical therapy in the hospital, she was allowed to leave during portions of the day. On a break, she and JP drove to church and decided that day to fully commit their lives to Jesus. That's when Lindsey decided she wanted to be baptized. Several men and JP helped carry her into the water where Ed baptized her. It was a beautiful illustration of the church caring for one of its own in crisis, and the church rallied around Lindsey and JP as they embarked on the long journey ahead.

Fast-forward two and a half years and you'll see Lindsey and her family walk through the doors of our church every Sunday. That's right, they all *walk*. After months of hard work in rehab, Lindsey miraculously regained the ability to walk.

Recently, we spoke with Lindsey and JP, and they shared how their intimacy with God deepened during this season. Because of that, their relationship with each other is stronger than ever and their newfound confidence in Christ has given them numerous opportunities to encourage others through their own seemingly hopeless times. The path through pain and the road to recovery ahead is still long, but the intimacy they have developed with God and their faith in him are their greatest sources of strength. Lindsey told us,

> Once we were all in, we never stopped leaning into Jesus and his church. God always provided what we needed at just the right time and made something beautiful out of one of the most painful situations in which someone could find themselves. It's taken us twenty-nine months to see the beauty. I don't understand why it happened to us—to me—but I do know that God's purpose is greater than any of us could ever understand! We can't see any other way we would be who we are today if we had not gone through this. We are so grateful to God for how close he is to us, and so hopeful for the future.

Recently, Lindsey did something she never thought she would be able to do again. With her three daughters cheering her on, she slid down the zip line at our church's camp and retreat center, Allaso Ranch. Afterward, her body and voice shaking, she said through tears of triumph, "I just want people to know that they can make it through hard things too."

God's All-Sufficient Grace

Have you ever tried to snap a selfie in a windstorm? Unless you're bald or have a buzz cut, that's never a pretty picture.

And if our hair reflected what we've been through in the storms of life, many of us would probably be walking around with a hat on.

Job would have had to wear a hat for sure. In addition to Job, someone else in the Bible would have had a windblown look. Someone who knew about the storms of life—and literal storms too. The apostle Paul not only was caught in storms while sailing the seas but also was shipwrecked—not once, not twice, but three times. Paul knew firsthand about the need for proper floatation devices. And he knew about the importance of having faith in God to see him through.

In his second letter to the church at Corinth, Paul listed some of the storms he'd endured: He had been put in prison for teaching about Jesus; he was whipped and beaten, and five times received the thirty-nine lashes; he was near death multiple times and even stoned. He survived three shipwrecks and once spent twenty-four hours adrift at sea. He lived in constant danger wherever he traveled. He often went without sleep, was hungry and thirsty, and lacked adequate shelter and clothing (2 Corinthians 11:23–27).

Wow. Paul knew pain. Whipped? Stoned? Three shipwrecks? Paul's life sounds like it was more storm than calm. More hurt than health. More stress than rest. But that's not all. After Paul listed all the ways he'd suffered, he talked about a chronic ailment, something he had suffered from for a long time. We're never told exactly what caused Paul so much pain, but after reading all he'd been through, are we surprised he had a chronic condition? Paul said he asked

God three times to take away his pain—to heal him. Here is what God said: "My grace is all you need, for my power is greatest when you are weak" (2 Corinthians 12:9 GNT). And Paul accepted that. He said,

> I am most happy, then, to be proud of my weaknesses, in order to feel the protection of Christ's power over me. I am content with weaknesses, insults, hardships, persecutions, and difficulties for Christ's sake. For when I am weak, then I am strong. (2 Corinthians 12:9–10 GNT)

Shipwrecked? God's grace was all Paul needed.

Beaten by Roman soldiers? God's grace was all Paul needed.

Betrayed by false friends? God's grace was all Paul needed.

Hungry? Homeless? God's grace was all Paul needed.

Life in immediate danger? God's grace was all Paul needed.

Through it all, God's grace was all Paul needed. God leveraged Paul's pain to intimately connect with him in the midst of his storms and struggles.

He Is the Right-Now God

Our son, EJ, was about four months old when we found out he had neurofibromatosis. He was born in the early nineties, so the internet wasn't really a thing yet. People didn't have computers in their homes. We couldn't open

WebMD or google "neurofibromatosis." When we shared EJ's diagnosis with our church, some members of our congregation went to a medical library to do some research for us. Honestly, we were terrified. After having LeeBeth, we'd suffered a miscarriage and secondary infertility. Then we waited five long years for God to bless us with this precious baby boy, and now he was sick?

It seemed cruel. The information we could scrape together wasn't encouraging. At the time EJ's condition was diagnosed it was thought to be the same as the "Elephant Man's Disease" and came with the possibility of extreme disfiguration. I (Lisa) remember Ed taking a call from his brother, Ben. Ben is a cerebral type, very smart. He is a student of Greek and Hebrew, and he shared something about the words God spoke to the apostle Paul when he was suffering: "My grace is sufficient for you, for my power is made perfect in weakness" (2 Corinthians 12:9 NIV).

"Ed, this verse is written in the present tense," Ben said. "That means God's grace is sufficient for you right now. In this moment. And five minutes from now? It'll be sufficient for you then. When you wake up in the morning, the grace of God will still be sufficient. It's a *right-now* verse." God knew exactly what we needed and when we needed it.

When Ed got off the phone, he looked stunned. He'd read that verse hundreds of times. He'd even preached on it. But this was the first time it truly came alive for him.

God's promise is in the present tense for you as well. If you are facing some high winds right now, be encouraged— you are in great company. Some of the greatest champions for Christ have been storm-tossed on high seas. They've had windblown hair. They've had stories of shipwrecks. But through it all, they stayed anchored to Christ. They stayed connected to heaven by the power of his Word. They knew God wasn't their enemy or the source of the storm. They knew him to be their life preserver—their Savior and security. He was intimately aware of their pain and chose to glorify himself through it while drawing closer to them. His grace is sufficient for all.

Have you been viewing God as the enemy? Has he been the target of your blame? Or has he been your source of strength during life's storms?

When Jesus is your anchor, you can be certain that God is not your enemy, but rather he is your security and offers you intimacy. His grace is sufficient for you.

Take a Step

FOUR STEPS ON THE PATH THROUGH PAIN

1. Admit you cannot process pain on your own.

2. *Believe Jesus is your loving Lord and anchor.*

3. Choose him daily to lead you by the hand.

4. Discover hope and healing in community.

- Which of Job's losses do you relate to most? Which of his responses? Write down some of the words Job said to

God that are similar to words you have said.

- On a scale of "Why me?" to "What now?" where are you on your journey? On the following line, draw an X to indicate your position.

  _____

  WHY ME?   **WHAT NOW?**

- What patterns of thought and behavior would you have to change to move you farther from "Why me?" and closer to "What now?" Write down at least three ways you can move farther down the line.

CHAPTER 5

I Surrender

God is carrying our hearts.
He alone sustains us with his
supernatural peace.

—Lisa's journal, one week
after LeeBeth's passing

I (Lisa) don't do bugs. I mean, only entomologists really *do* bugs, but I really, really don't do bugs. Recently, I was standing in my yard watching my grandchildren play when, out of the corner of my eye, I saw something dark emerge from the grass and begin to crawl across the sidewalk. I'll be the first to admit that my eyesight is not what it used to be, but I do wear glasses. And I'm telling you, as I live and breathe, that what crawled onto my sidewalk was the largest beetle ever to crawl under the heavens.

"Ed! A bug!" I whisper-screamed. I didn't want to alert the grandkids to the intruder in our midst. Ed looked down and even his eyes grew wide. I'll let him pick up the story from here.

I (Ed) can confirm Lisa's assessment that this beetle was the gargantuan emperor of all beetles. You want to talk about tough? It was almost like I could see his triceps and biceps flex as his little feet hit the pavement. He wasn't scurrying or trying to get away from me. No, he was marching ahead like he had somewhere to be. His swagger said, "This is my sidewalk. This is my yard. I am going to walk where I please." Even when I moved into the beetle's path and got down face-to-face with him, he didn't bear to the left or to the right; he kept coming straight at me.

I called over my shoulder to Lisa, "You know what? This beetle doesn't know who he's messing with." He didn't know how powerful I was. I was a human being and many times his size. But in his little beetle brain he thought, "I'm going to forge my own path. I'm going to do my own thing."

Perhaps you can see where this story is going, but I'll go ahead and say it. If an analogy were made about the difference between humans and God, we'd be the beetle and God would be the human. God has all the power. God has unlimited power, and our power isn't even a bug's whisper in comparison.

Power Play

In my standoff with the beetle, I could have changed pretty much anything I wanted to about that bug's life. I could have gotten a little aquarium and set it up with the juiciest, greenest leaves a beetle could ever want. I could have scooped him up and taken him to the edge of the yard to relocate him away from my wife and grandkids. And, yes, I could have literally stamped out his life. I had all the power and he had none.

In the same way, God has all the power here on earth and in heaven. He is *omnipotent*. *Omni* is a prefix that means "all"; *potent* is related to power—so God is all-powerful. While I had power over the beetle, I wasn't *all*-powerful; I couldn't have spoken a word and made the beetle jump or fly. But God could. God's power is so limitless that our finite minds can't even begin to comprehend it.

As with my standoff with the beetle, there have been times I have come face-to-face with God in a standoff. You probably have too. We have seen God standing in our path and we've imagined that we somehow know better, that we have access to something or someone more powerful than he is. Maybe we even think that power source is ourselves. We are especially prone to make this kind of power play when we're in pain. We think, "God caused this thing that's making life painful, so I don't want anything to do with God. Instead, I'm going to rely on _____." Fill in the blank with your coping mechanism of choice.

But the Bible—our survival guide—tells us to do something very different. If we're anchored in the Lord, if we're making daily deposits in our relationship with him and staying in his Word, we already know we're to rely on God's

power in times of crisis, pain, and struggle. The prophet
Isaiah wrote,

> Don't you know? Haven't you heard?
> The LORD is the everlasting God;
>> he created all the world.
> He never grows tired or weary.
>> No one understands his thoughts.
> He strengthens those who are weak and tired.
> Even those who are young grow weak;
>> young people can fall exhausted.
> But those who trust in the LORD for help
>> will find their strength renewed.
> They will rise on wings like eagles;
>> they will run and not get weary;
>> they will walk and not grow weak.
>> (Isaiah 40:28–31 GNT)

Isaiah wasn't just talking about raw power, he was talking about true power. It takes no more energy for God to
create a universe than it does for him to create a mosquito.
God's power is unlimited. He never grows tired or weary.

God can and will renew our strength and give us the
ability to carry on even when we think we can't take one
more step. God's strength becomes our strength when we
reach for him in our moments of pain. When we tap into
him as our power source, he will restore our hope. And we
learn to do that when we take our next step in the four steps
on the path through pain.

Step 3: Choose Him Daily to Lead You by the Hand

As a reminder, the path through pain isn't linear. There are ups and downs. One good day might be followed by a week of bad days. When we surrender our weariness, pain, and struggle to Jesus, we will find strength, rest, peace, and even joy. They can all coexist even in a broken heart as we walk hand in hand with Christ, relying on him minute by minute. On this journey toward healing, step 3 is the step over which you have the most control. This is the step that leads you back to truth when the whispered lies of the Enemy threaten to overwhelm you. When you're in pain and you don't know what to do, step 3 is the answer: choose Jesus daily to lead you by the hand. God isn't going to give you all the puzzle pieces to your future in advance, but we are confident he will reveal what you need to do in each moment at the very moment you need to do it. But first you need to give him your hand. You need to say, "I surrender to you, Jesus." This often becomes a daily, if not an hour-by-hour, minute-by-minute, decision to surrender and accept that you can't do this alone. It is a decision to relinquish control and request his help.

We fight against relinquishing control, don't we? We want to *understand*. We want *answers*. And we want the pain to go away! We want life to stop hurting. We want to get back what we lost. We want to rewind five minutes, five days, five years. We want what we want, when we want it. But what if what God wants is better than what we want?

Shouldn't we trust his will and his way—even when it differs from ours?

People sometimes ask me (Lisa), "How are you? Really—how have things been since LeeBeth passed?" That answer is complicated. In many ways, it has been absolute darkness. An abyss of ache. A black hole of breaking, over and over again. But simultaneously, since January 19, 2021, I have experienced the richest walk in this pathway through pain. My connection with Jesus has been magnetized. I am glued to his side like an anxious child in a crowd of strangers might be to her father.

My favorite Christmas carol is "O Holy Night." And my favorite line in the song is "A thrill of hope, the weary world rejoices." Yes, our world is *weary*. Why? Because this is not a happy-ending world, a perfect world, or a that-unspeakable-tragedy-didn't-really-happen world. This line acknowledges that we will face weariness.

But this weary world can also *rejoice* because Jesus is *here*. Regardless of my situation, regardless of my pain, regardless of my sorrow—I can rejoice in my weariness because I am not alone in my pain. What a thrill of hope that hope is!

Often, being joyous is hard. I choose joy because I know that Jesus is my Savior and my source of joy. I don't rejoice in my circumstances or because of my circumstances; I rejoice because of who he is. This is my certain hope, even though it is not yet fully seen or understood. Every day I am challenged to act out these verses, over and over:

I lift up my eyes to the mountains—
　　where does my help come from?
My help comes from the LORD,
　　the Maker of heaven and earth.
　　　　(Psalm 121:1–2 NIV)

We must always remember that we are able to rejoice only when we surrender control to Jesus.

God's Power Has a Purpose

I (Ed) am going to reveal three things right now that I have never in my life revealed. This is a true confession. I, Pastor Ed Young, can bench-press 3,500 pounds. I can! Secondly, I have a vertical jump of six feet. And last, but certainly not least, I can hit a golf ball 800 yards.

Do you believe me? No? Well, guess what—you're *wrong*. Your thinking is too limited because you're considering only what's possible on earth. All I have to do to accomplish these three feats is hop aboard a spaceship and get dropped off on the moon. Then you could turn on the television and be amazed at what I, Pastor Ed Young, could do. *Wow!* He's bench pressing 3,500 pounds. He's making a six-foot vertical jump—and in a space suit too! Is that a sand wedge? *Swish.* One-handed.

You didn't believe I could do all those things because you limited the realm of possibilities to earth. But the laws of gravity are different on the moon. The calculus of what's possible changes because the moon is a whole different realm.

The analogy of what's possible on the moon gives us an inkling of what's possible with the unlimited, omnipotent power of God. He is infinite. His ways are not our ways, and his thoughts are not our thoughts (Isaiah 55:8–9). He's in another realm. So when we try to use our limited human reasoning to imagine what's possible with an omnipotent God, our minds fail us. Relatively speaking, we're like beetles on a sidewalk. We have to learn how to treat God like God. Which means we need to remember that God's power is not only far beyond our own, but it also always has a purpose.

We can never detach God's omnipotence from his sovereignty. With God, it's never a question of whether he has power, but rather how his power aligns with his will. Or, more specifically, whether our will aligns with his. That's why the night before Jesus died, he prayed to the Father, "Not my will, but yours be done" (Luke 22:42 NIV).

Our lives aren't meant to be about our will—about going our own way in our own power. Remember, we have the will and power of a beetle compared to God's. Instead, our lives are meant to be about trusting that God knows what's best for us. And on our path through pain, we do that by allowing him to lead us by the hand. We trust he has our best interests at heart even when our beetle brains think we know better.

If you have kids, you may have experienced the same kind of power play, especially as they get older and the stakes get higher. Sometimes they are convinced you either don't know or don't care what's best for them. And when they don't get what they want? Oh man. Their pain is *big*. "Everyone else's parents let them . . ." The pain is all they can think about because in their beetle brains, what they want makes sense. It's so obvious! But you have more information. You have more context for the purpose in their pain. You know what's best. And it's no different with our omnipotent heavenly Father. He wields his power purposefully, according to his will.

After we processed the initial shock of LeeBeth's death, I (Lisa) tried to move from "Why me?" to "What now?" I knew that shift was not only what God asked of me but also the only way I could begin to heal. Any by "heal," I don't mean that the pain would go away. I don't believe there will ever be a day I wake up on this earth and do not experience the ache of losing my daughter. Healing isn't the absence of hurt; healing is the presence of peace. If I wanted peace, I knew I had to have some difficult conversations with God.

In my prayers and journaling, I found myself asking, "God, what is the purpose in all this? If you could reveal to me why LeeBeth had to be taken so soon, I could make peace with it." I was obsessed with trying to align my logic with God's logic. It was during one of these times in prayer that I had a thought: "If I truly understood God's logic, I wouldn't want LeeBeth back."

I immediately rejected that thought. There's nothing I could learn about losing LeeBeth that would make me not want her back here with us. But then conviction struck me right in the gut. This verse came to mind: "But who are you, my friend, to talk back to God?" (Romans 9:20 GNT). *Who are you, Lisa, to talk back to God? Who are you to say, "Well, if I knew . . ." about anything? Are you purporting to know God's purpose more intimately than God himself? Are you asserting that God's purpose can't be bigger than your pain?*

That's when I had to repent of my mindset. "Not my will, Father," I prayed, "but yours. You are all-knowing, all-loving, and all-powerful." I may not have always felt that prayer in my heart, but the more I prayed it, the more my actions followed it. And the more my actions followed it, the more my heart did too. On that day, and the days that followed, reaching for the hand of God looked a lot like a trust fall. I did it over and over, sometimes with confidence. Other times with blind faith.

Power and Faith

Have you ever watched a late-night infomercial where the host is selling something like a knife set or a refrigerator storage system? You know, the ones where they give you a "limited-time offer" of a low, low price? Then, just when you think they're going to stop haggling you, the shot zooms in on the host's face right before they declare, "Wait! There's more!"

Well, we're not trying to come off as a cheesy infomercial here, but when it comes to the power of God . . . Wait! There's more!

Not only is God all-powerful, but God has made the

sovereign choice to share his power with weak individuals like us. And he doesn't just *want* to share it, he is *eager* to give it to us. He can't wait to see us use it. He can't wait to watch it revolutionize our lives and the lives of the people around us. The passage we shared earlier from Isaiah tells us exactly how we can receive the gift of God's power: "Those who trust in the LORD for help will find their strength renewed" (Isaiah 40:31 GNT).

I (Ed) have heard it said, "God is omnipotent. He wants to share his power with you. His power will change your life." And that's true. I have read it in the Bible. I have taken notes when other pastors taught on it. I have gone to seminary and done some doctoral work on it. But sometimes I still find myself saying, "God, I believe you are omnipotent. But I don't know how much that omnipotence finds its way into my life on earth." That's especially true when I'm hurting. I don't feel powerful. Instead, I feel the complete opposite. And I'm guessing you can relate. So if God gives us access to his power, why don't we always experience it in tangible ways? What's the problem?

Although there might be any number of reasons, I think the most common one is a lack of faith. A lack of faith keeps God's omnipotence from being released in our lives. What is faith? The author of Hebrews tells us, "Now faith is confidence in what we hope for and assurance about what we do not see" (Hebrews 11:1 NIV). I have also heard it said that faith is walking to the edge of where the light meets the darkness and taking one more step. That one more step is how we demonstrate that we really do trust the One who is in control.

As I read the Bible, I am blown away by this pattern: *The power of God is not released until someone takes a risky step of faith.* We see it clearly in the exodus story, when Moses led the children of Israel out of slavery in Egypt. Hundreds of thousands of people followed him. A visible manifestation of God—a cloud—led them. They were walking along with Moses when the cloud pointed them toward the Red Sea. I'm sure Moses was thinking, "What, God? The Red Sea? Have you hidden thousands of boats nearby?" Don't forget that the Egyptians were following closely behind, and they were mad and mean. I imagine Moses looking from the cloud to the sea, from the sea to the people, from the people back to the cloud.

Here's what happened next: "The LORD said to Moses, 'Why are you crying out for help? Tell the people to move forward'" (Exodus 14:15 GNT). So Moses made a risky move and put his size thirteen (I'm guessing) sandal next to the water. I can imagine the Red Sea lapping up on his toes as he took this step, which was a giant leap of faith. He extended his staff and *that's* when the waters parted—not when Moses stood on the shore looking up at the cloud, but when he took a step of obedience into the impossible. Suddenly, the waters separated, and the children of Israel crossed safely to the other side.

The pattern repeats itself in Joshua 3. Joshua was leading the Israelites to the Promised Land when they once again encountered an impassable water hazard, the Jordan River. I know the Jordan River well because I've baptized people in it—and its waters are frigid. The Lord told Joshua to give these instructions to the priests carrying the ark of the covenant: "When you reach the edge of the Jordan's waters, go and stand in the river" (Joshua 3:8 NIV). Here's what happened: "As soon as the priests stepped into the river, the water stopped flowing and piled up, far upstream at Adam, the city beside Zarethan. The flow downstream to the Dead Sea was completely cut off, and the people were able to cross over near Jericho" (Joshua 3:15–16 GNT).

Did you catch that? "As soon as the priests stepped into the river." The river didn't dry up until they stepped into it. Until they took a step of faith. Until they acted courageously. Only then did God perform the miracle that enabled them to cross through the treacherous waters.

God's power is unleashed when we take a step of faith. Which means the secret to unlocking and unleashing the power of God in our lives is to first acknowledge our weakness. In our weakness we say, "God, I can't, but you can. I'm not in control, and I am not all-powerful. You are God; I am not. I will trust you by taking a risky first step."

That's why step 3 in processing pain requires faith-based action. Choosing God daily to lead you by the hand is no small thing. It's not a throw-up-a-prayer-and-hope-for-the-best mentality. It's a disciplined and risky choice—sometimes an hourly one! But it's also how we plug into the power of God and experience peace when we're in pain and face crippling challenges.

What might it look like for you to put your foot in the water, to take one risky step? Does it look like finally signing up for counseling? Ending a relationship? Resigning from your job? Putting down the bottle and attending an AA meeting? Walking back through the doors of a church?

After LeeBeth's passing, I (Lisa) felt like simply being out in public was a risky step of faith. It was a confusing and conflicting experience because I knew people were watching how Ed and I were processing our pain. We had preached for years about the goodness of God, and I knew some were thinking, "Let's see how good their God is now. Let's see how they handle this. Let's see if they implode." It was a lot of pressure. I remember being at LeeBeth's memorial service and thinking, "Am I a pastor here, or a parishioner? Am I supposed to be comforting others, or are they supposed to be comforting me?" I felt the weight of the world's eyes on us. Every time I walked out the door, I had to pray, "Lord, hold me together. I don't want to be fake, but I don't want people to doubt our faith—to doubt that we believe you are able."

It's easy to trust God when things are going our way, but the true test is our willingness to take a faith-filled step into the unknown when it seems like nothing is going our way. When we're in pain and long to experience God's power, it's time to put our feet in the water. It is an act of *faith*, not *feeling*.

God's Miraculous Power

A remarkable man in our church has a story that speaks to our questions about God's miraculous power today. This is how his son tells it.

My dad was diagnosed with cancer in the summer of 2020. I wanted to pray and believe in miracles, but I also wanted to prepare myself for the possibility that he might not come through. I started praying prayers that were bolder than I'd ever prayed. But then, three months later, my father died.

I was angry. I was confused. I was questioning God. Why didn't we get the miracle we prayed for? Then I began to look around and see all these other miracles we did receive. I probably have more memories from that last year of his life than my whole childhood growing up. Memories with meaningful conversations of love and wisdom that have made a mark on who I am as a husband and a father, as a man. From the last year all the way up to the moment he passed away, being in the hospital with him, we got to pray over him, we got to worship in the room with him, and we were able to give him comfort and peace as he took those final steps toward eternity. *That's* a miracle.

My dad had a crazy past and had things happen to him that are incredibly unfair and painful—a lot of abuse. It would have been very easy for him to repeat those patterns in his own family. But my dad was not the byproduct of his past; he was the byproduct of a relationship with Jesus. *That's* a miracle. The amount of forgiveness that flowed from that man, the amount of joy and positivity—it could only be possible by Jesus's miraculous healing love.

I know that there will be miracles I pray for that don't happen, but that doesn't change the fact that Jesus is still capable of miracles. He's already done the greatest miracle, coming from heaven to earth to give his life for me and for you. *That's* a miracle. Rising from the grave three days later? *That's* a miracle. Offering us an eternity with him if we will simply believe it and receive it? *That's* a miracle. Saving us by his grace through faith? *That's* a miracle. And so that's what my story is all about—praying and believing for miracles, but also resting in the greatest miracle that he's already done.

Our Father is still on the throne. Though we may wrestle with pain, though we may not get the miracle we pray for, his power is not diminished. He still says, "I'm in control," because he is still God.

God's Power Is Transformational

Once we tap into the power of God, we will begin to change. Our hearts, our minds, and even our pain will change because the power of God is transformational. But remember, God's power is often withheld until we take a step of faith. So what does it look like to take a step of faith in everyday life? Let us explain it with an example we can probably all relate to.

You're driving home from work and you feel low because it was a terrible, horrible, no good, very bad day. Everything went wrong, and you know as soon as your feet cross the threshold, your spouse will want to talk to you, but you don't want to talk. You know the kids will be asking you to play games with them, but you don't feel like managing their expectations either. You just want to collapse onto the sofa and watch mind-numbing TV with no one bothering you.

Have you ever felt that way? We have. But Isaiah wrote that we could soar on wings like eagles (Isaiah 40:31). When we feel more like a wounded duck instead, we have a choice to make. Either we can act on the way we feel, or we can act on who God says we are and trust that the feelings will follow. That's when we decide to believe, in faith, that "those who trust in the LORD for help will find their strength renewed" (Isaiah 40:31 GNT).

God's power is unlimited, purposeful, and transformational, and it is available to you in every moment. To access that power, you decide to be like Moses and Joshua and take a step of faith. You make the choice to greet your spouse warmly. You make the choice to look into your kids' eyes when they talk to you. You make the choice to respond with genuine affection, not with gritted teeth. By the transformative power of God within you, you don't put your family in pain just because you're in pain. That's God's power at work in you.

You take that step of faith, and the power of God

energizes you. You're amazed as his power changes your attitude and mindset. Then the vise grip of defeat around your heart begins to loosen. With every choice you make, you are taking steps into the water. You are parting the Red Sea of your pain and walking through it to the other side.

This is how we take God's hand daily and choose him to lead us. It is an act of faith—acting like it is so, even when it doesn't feel so, in order that it may be so. We can access God's power, but it takes action to create traction.

What or whom are you choosing to lead you daily? Would you be willing to take God's hand right now, to move forward into whatever seems impossible for you? God's power is available to you, and it can transform you, one risky step at a time.

Take a Step

FOUR STEPS ON THE PATH THROUGH PAIN

1. Admit you cannot process pain on your own.

2. Believe Jesus is your loving Lord and anchor.

3. *Choose him daily to lead you by the hand.*

4. Discover hope and healing in community.

- Are you prepared to take step 3 on the path through pain? What patterns of thought or behavior would you have to change to take that step?

- What step of faith might God be asking you to take to unleash his power? Are you willing to take that risky step?

- Set a reminder on your phone to go off at the same time each morning. Label the reminder something like "Take God's hand." Whenever that reminder goes off, set your heart on taking God's hand. Maybe for you that means praying a prayer of surrender like this one:

  Lord, today I choose to walk in your steps. As you lead me, I don't want to walk this path alone. I want you to be my guide. You are the only one who can make my path manageable. Your power will strengthen me to take each step through my pain. I trust you, Jesus.

  Maybe it means reciting a verse you have memorized. For example,

  Trust in the LORD with all your heart
      and lean not on your own understanding;
  in all your ways submit to him,
      and he will make your paths straight.
          (Proverbs 3:5–6 NIV)

  Maybe it means reaching out to someone and allowing them to encourage or pray for you.

CHAPTER 6

Is God Good?

Our grief is so deep, but as Corrie ten Boom quoted her sister Betsie (during the Nazi occupation), "There is no pit so deep that God is not deeper still." Your power, Lord, is what sustains us.

—Lisa's journal, three weeks
after LeeBeth's passing

LeeBeth passed away on January 19, 2021. Six months later, on June 23, 2021, I (Ed) was leaving a meeting when I had an encounter in a parking lot. I wrote down the date in my Bible because what happened next was a conversation I didn't ever want to forget.

I was trying to find my car. I've been known to be directionally challenged, so my predicament wasn't an anomaly. I had just spotted it some distance away when I heard someone behind me call my name. I turned and saw Bart, whom I've known for several years and who'd also been in the meeting I'd just left. I assumed I'd left something behind and he was walking out to return it to me.

But when Bart approached, I noticed he had tears in his eyes and his lip was trembling. "I'm so sorry to hear about your daughter," he said. We hadn't discussed LeeBeth's death in the meeting, so now I figured he'd followed me so he could offer his condolences.

Wrong again.

"I can't imagine the pain you're going through," he said.

His words touched me. "Bart, you're so kind. Thank you for that. It's been a nightmare." Then I added, "But along with this nightmare track we've been on—along with the pain—there's another track of joy we've experienced. And, quite frankly, we've seen the goodness of God in new and unexpected ways. I can't explain it, but that's where we are right now."

Then Bart pivoted the conversation, which revealed the real reason he'd followed me into the parking lot. "I have these friends," he said. "They're wonderful people. And they have three young kids. This family is wonderful, but they're going through something awful."

Ah, now I see where this is going. As a pastor, I can usually sense when someone has a challenge to God's goodness. Bart was hurting, crying out for answers, and searching to make sense of the pain he saw this family going through.

He went on to explain that the father, who was in his thirties, had recently been diagnosed with amyotrophic lateral sclerosis (ALS), or Lou Gehrig's disease. As diseases go, ALS is horrific, usually leading to a slow and painful death.

"Not only that," Bart said, "but his wife just had a double mastectomy." Yes, while the husband was battling ALS, the wife was suffering from breast cancer. Again, this couple had three little kids, and both parents had life-threatening illnesses.

Then Bart broke down and began to cry—and this guy is not a crier. He's what you might call a man's man. He said, "If God allows something like that to happen to people who are good, I don't want to play on his team."

He was telling me all this in a parking lot on a day when it was about ninety-eight degrees, and I was wearing a suit. Now I was sweating in every possible way. *God, what do I say?* It was a quick, microwave prayer. *What do I say to Bart?*

What would you have said to Bart? What would you have said about the goodness of God in the face of such injustice?

We've addressed this issue of suffering and God's goodness in bits and pieces in previous chapters, but now we're going to zoom in and take a closer look. Because if we're going to follow through on step 3—to choose God daily to lead us by the hand—we need to be clear about a fundamental truth: before the pain hits, we must believe that God is, in fact, good.

In the pages that follow, we'll explore some biblical truths about the goodness of God. And here's a spoiler alert for what we're about to discover: God is good when things are good. God is good when things are bad. Because God is innately good. Then I'll give you the CliffsNotes version of how I responded to Bart in the parking lot that day. I believe my response to him was led by the Holy Spirit of God—because some of the things I said surprised even me! In the end we will discover something incredible: God is good to us even when we don't deserve it. That is called grace. But first, we start with the fundamental truth that God is good.

God Is Good

God is good because he cannot be anything else. It's who he is. God is *intrinsically* good. The author of 1 and 2 Chronicles wrote, "Give thanks to the LORD, because he is good" (1 Chronicles 16:34 GNT). The psalmist proclaimed, "Find out for yourself how good the LORD is," and "Give thanks to him and praise him. The LORD is good" (Psalm 34:8; Psalm 100:4–5 GNT).

The psalmist also declared,

> How great is Your goodness
> that You have stored up for those who fear You
> and accomplished in the sight of everyone
> for those who take refuge in You.
> (Psalm 31:19–20 HCSB)

Isn't that cool? It's like the goodness of God is boxed up in a storage unit just waiting for us to claim it all.

As followers of Christ, we have access to God's goodness

because the God of the universe has it stored up specifically for those who take refuge in him. So why don't we always feel that goodness? To address that question, we need to take a step back and consider the bigger picture of God's goodness, which is his plan to save the world. We need to understand four foundational truths about God's goodness and our own: we're good only if we're perfect, God can transfer all of his goodness to us, God covers us because he is good, and God's goodness doesn't always look good to us.

WE'RE GOOD ONLY IF WE'RE PERFECT

We've all heard of the Hall of Fame in sports. Only the most elite, top-performing athletes have the honor of being named into this exclusive collection of players. It's an incredible honor. But do you know what *doesn't* exist in sports? The Hall of Perfection. To be inducted into the Hall of Perfection, you'd have to play a perfect game. Zero mistakes or errors—even in practice.

Guess who would qualify for the Hall of Perfection. No one. Not a single player, past or present, has played perfectly their entire career. Not even close!

The Bible says there are two ways to get into heaven. Did you know that? Not one, but two. The first one is the Hall of Perfection strategy. If you're perfect, if you're perfectly good, at the end of your life, God will say, "Okay, you earned your way in." You could call that Plan A. But most of us know that Plan A doesn't work. I mean, if I were trying to be perfect, I blew that a long time ago. So did you. I don't care if you get baptized a hundred times a day. I don't care if you give all your money to charity. I don't care if you're the most moral man or woman around. The Bible says, you will still fall short of God's standard of perfection and will miss out on heaven.

Since Plan A isn't an option, our good God went to work to create a Plan B—a plan to solve the sin problem he didn't create. Plan B places the weight and hope of our lives on the death and resurrection of Jesus Christ. His goodness carries us.

GOD CAN TRANSFER ALL OF HIS GOODNESS TO US

Only Jesus can take all our badness and give us all of his goodness through the redemptive work he did on the cross. (See "Jesus's Rescue Plan" in chapter 4, pages 46–49). To give you a picture of what that looks like, here is an incredible story that demonstrates the transformative power of God's grace, mercy, and redemption.

Ashley's choices had cost her everything. By the age of fourteen, she was addicted to drugs and worked as a prostitute to support her habit. In her twenties she was already on a hopeless path filled with arrests, times in and out of prison, and failed stints in rehab. She had been physically assaulted and had woken up in ambulances. She had lost her kids because of the mess she made of her life.

When Ashley began searching for a way to turn her life around in 2012, she started going to church, but she was still in a full-on battle with addiction. She felt welcomed and loved at our church and would experience moments of victory, but then she'd relapse. Her ex-husband tried to kill her when she was pregnant with her daughter, and that sent her into a terrifying downward spiral of anxiety and depression. Then, in 2018, her family attended the Christmas service, and Ashley gave her life to Jesus.

"He forgave me," she said. "My sins were gone. I felt like a weight was gone off my chest! Turning my life around has been the hardest thing I have ever had to do. But I haven't done it alone. Fellowship Church has helped me surround myself with the right people who encourage me, equip me, and empower me through Jesus and his Word."

Ashley's story is truly an amazing grace story. God's goodness met Ashley right where she was, trapped in a life that was in shambles from sin. The same good God who provided a way for a rejected Samaritan woman to meet the Savior, also met Ashley.

Grace extends God's goodness to those who don't deserve it—to all of us, including you and me. His grace redeems and restores. God, in his lovingkindness, looks at us and sees Jesus. The grace of God heals our broken, bruised souls and releases us from the hold of sin. It sets us free to live a life empowered by the Holy Spirit.

GOD COVERS US BECAUSE HE IS GOOD

In a recent rereading of the encounter between God and his creations, Adam and Eve, I noticed a tender moment. Adam and Eve had eaten the forbidden fruit and realized, for the first time, that they were naked. They heard God walking in the garden, so they hid.

"Where are you?" God asked (Genesis 3:9 NIV).

"I heard you in the garden," Adam responded. "I was afraid because I was naked; so I hid" (Genesis 3:10 NIV).

God knew Adam and Eve had disobeyed him. He knew they had eaten from the one tree he told them not to eat from. Can you imagine how heartbroken God must have been? If you're a parent, you know that sickening drop in your gut when your children disobey a rule you set to protect them. It's so painful.

Life was different for Adam and Eve from the moment they received their first set of punishments, including removal from their home in paradise. But God took a tender and loving action in the midst of all the upheaval: "The LORD God made clothes out of animal skins for Adam and his wife, and he clothed them" (Genesis 3:21 GNT).

Isn't that just like a loving parent? Isn't that better than how most of us would have responded? If it had been my kids and I realized they were naked because they broke my *one* rule, I would have said, "Good luck figuring out clothes, guys. Since you obviously know better than I do what's good for you, go ahead. You're on your own."

But that isn't what our good God did. Even after Adam and Eve disobeyed, God literally covered them. He fashioned clothes for them from animal skins to remove some of the sting of their shame. It wasn't a problem he created, but he found a solution. Just as he did with our salvation.

Sometimes people will ask, "Well, why did God give us the option to choose evil? Why not make everyone good?" God made us with a free will because of love. Love can't be forced or coerced, and God wanted us to freely choose to love him. With free will, we can choose to follow the right way, the goodness of God, or we can choose to go a direction that takes us away from God. Evil is simply the absence of the goodness of God.

You might be thinking, "Can you stop talking about this already? I get it—God is good." But do you *feel* and *believe* that God is good? Can you separate your pain from your opinion of God?

I (Ed) have 26,200 photos on my phone—a decade's worth of pictures dating back to 2012. But even if you went to the beginning of my camera roll and looked at every photo, you wouldn't have a full picture of who I am and all I've been through. In the same way, you couldn't review all my posts on social media and say, "Oh, that's Ed's life story. That's a clear description of who Ed is and what he's about." No, if you were to study me, you'd have to go all the way back to the beginning of my life—to that first squinty-eyed, swollen-faced photo of newborn me in the hospital.

To fully understand somebody, we need to know the full context of their lives. But far too often, we see just four or five snapshots of God and think, "That's God." We hear a few painful stories or experience a few painful moments of our own, and we form our opinion of God on those moments alone. But to begin to understand God, we need a much bigger photo album. We need to zoom way, way out, farther back in human history than we can even see, to gain a better perspective of who God is.

GOD'S GOODNESS DOESN'T
ALWAYS LOOK GOOD TO US

There's a segment of the Christian community that focuses heavily on the ideas of prosperity, faith, deliverance, and miracles. These are the most talked-about topics in their gatherings. And the underlying vibe is, if you're sick and you're not healed, you don't have enough faith. Well, that's heresy. I hope you know that. Whenever you hear that, know that it's not biblical.

God is not a genie who grants wishes, and faith is not the currency we use to get what we want from God. Is faith important? Yes. Does God perform miracles? Yes. Does he heal everybody in the way we think they should be healed? No. Quite frankly, most of the people I've prayed for in healing services over the years have since died. Yes, there are some miraculous turnarounds, but mostly, people with terminal diagnoses don't survive them.

One of the biggest problems we have with pain and what causes us to question God's goodness is that we don't have the full context for the goodness of God. We focus only on the handful of snapshots we have in front of us. When we're presented with a horrible situation or a heartbreaking circumstance, we're tempted to equate that reality to the quality of God's goodness. The truth is that the only snapshot required to gauge the goodness of God is the one of Jesus hanging on a cross, exchanging his perfection for our rags of sin, redeeming our futures for eternity. And God doesn't stop there. His goodness continues today to you and me in ways we can't imagine or fully understand. He desires to meet your needs daily, to carry you through the trials, tests, or temptations you face. His goodness is on tap to sustain you through every storm, struggle, or season of suffering. Though we are tempted to question God's goodness in times like these, it is in fact in times like these that his goodness is most relevant.

The Four Things I Said to Bart

I want to bring you back to earlier in this chapter—to me sweating rivers in a parking lot while Bart waited on my response to his question: "Why would I want to follow a God who allows bad things to happen to good people?" Now that I've established the inarguable truth that God is good, I want to share my response to Bart.

1. WE LIVE IN A FALLEN WORLD

I told Bart, "We live in a fallen world." And that means two things: our world is not perfect, and we are not good. Though I didn't get into much more detail with Bart, here are the implications of my words to him:

Our World Is Not Perfect

Our world is not perfect. Why? One word: sin. That's it. Why is our world fallen? Sin. It affects us directly and indirectly. We live in a world where bad things happen to good people and good things happen to bad people. The Bible says the rains fall on the just and the unjust alike (Matthew 5:45). Bad things happen. Why? Trace it all the way back to the day Adam and Eve ate forbidden fruit in the garden of Eden. Sin. S-I-N. And because of our inheritance of sin, which I call our sin-etics, we have a hard time discerning what or who is good.

We Are Not Good

Are we good? Not so much. On my best day, I fall miserably short on the goodness continuum because, unlike God, I am far from good. Like every other human being on the planet, I have a sin nature.

Human beings are not innately good. How do I know? For one, I am a human and I have met humans. On our own, we are not very good. And two, the Bible says so. Jesus said, "No one is good except God alone" (Mark 10:18 NASB). The apostle Paul wrote, "There is no one who is righteous" (Romans 3:10 GNT), and "All have sinned" (Romans 3:23 NIV). The evidence that we are not good is all around us.

Consider the popularity of a show like *Keeping Up with the Kardashians*, which had a twenty-year run on reality television, and now keeps going as *The Kardashians*. Why are many of us drawn to shows like this, which showcase dysfunction and a lack of moral fortitude? My theory is that we watch them because they make us feel better about ourselves. We think, "They're beautiful people and they spend more money in a month than I'll make in my lifetime, but I'm a much better person than they are. They have fame and fortune, but look how messed up they are." What does it say about us that we like watching them because it makes us feel better about ourselves?

Have you ever had lessons on how to compare yourself with others so you could feel superior? I doubt it. We aren't taught how to sin, it's simply *in* us. Obviously, our good isn't that good. And we don't have to look any further than the world around us for evidence of that—there is violence, poverty, abuse, crime, racism, and the list could keep going. The point is clear: we are not good.

2. THIS IS NOT ALL THERE IS

That's why I told Bart next, "This is not all there is. In walking through our grief, it's like Lisa and I are walking on two parallel tracks. We have joy and the goodness of God on one track, and then the pain and the nightmare of loss on the other."

If you've driven on any large interstates, you may have gotten in the high-occupancy vehicle lane (HOV) at some point. But there's still a regular lane right next to it, and the two lanes run parallel. Eventually, the HOV lane stops and the other lanes keep going. The Bible promises us that one day our pain and suffering will stop. Yet as Christ followers, we'll keep going and going.

"We don't know why God allows evil to exist," I said to Bart. "And we'll never know the answer until we move from this side of the dirt to the other. We're simply not going to know." And as we said before, even if God were to give us a reason, we probably wouldn't have the bandwidth to comprehend it.

On January 19, 2021, I brought LeeBeth to our house and put her in a room not far from my office. She was anxious—a common symptom of withdrawal from drugs and alcohol. I asked her if she needed anything. She said no. Then I said, "LeeBeth, I love you," and kissed her forehead.

Those were my last words to my daughter before I retreated to my office. In a matter of minutes, I heard a noise from the room. "LeeBeth?" I called. There was no answer. I rushed to her side—maybe five seconds after I heard the sound of what I now believe to be her seizure. By the time I entered the room, she was already mostly gone.

When you've been as close to someone dying as I have, you understand the brevity of life. But life is not the final chapter for any of us. We *all* live forever in one of two places—either the right place or the wrong place. Sometimes people ask, "Why would God create Satan? Why would a good God create evil?" The simple answer is, God didn't create evil. Evil is the consequence of choice. Satan's existence was birthed out of rebellion and rejection of God's authority. That's why Jesus said, "I saw Satan fall like lightning from heaven" (Luke 10:18 NIV). Satan rebelled and was cast out. He chose to disobey God and now suffers the consequences for all eternity.

Yes, what happens here on earth will end for every single one of us. But there's eternity on the other side, and it's your choice what that eternity looks like. Death isn't the end of the game. Our pain isn't the end of the game. What's happening in our lives, whatever it is and however cruel it can feel, isn't the end of the game.

3. THE WORST THING HAPPENED
TO THE BEST PERSON

"The worst thing happened to the best person: Jesus," I said to Bart. I'm convinced God gave me these words, because I'm not that smart. But have you ever thought about this? That the worst things that could ever happen did in fact happen to the best person who ever lived?

Let your mind go back to the scenes of Jesus's final days on earth. He was betrayed and abandoned by his closet friends, wrongfully imprisoned, tortured, and humiliated; and then our good God, who can't even look at sin, poured out his wrath, his justice, and his judgment on his own Son. Jesus willingly took on the punishment we deserve—the worst thing that could ever happen—because he was the best person ever to walk the earth.

When we, like Bart, wrestle with the question, "Why do bad things happen to good people?" this is the only appropriate response: sin. That's also why the worst thing happened to the best person—but, more specifically, that happened because of *our sin*. If we used logic to try to determine what's "fair," we'd have to go all the way back to the cross. What Jesus did for us there was anything but fair—it was the personification of mercy and grace. The earth does spin on the axis of justice, and we should be grateful for that.

4. GOD LEVERAGES PAIN IN POWERFUL
AND MYSTERIOUS WAYS

The last thing I said to Bart is perhaps the most important. I said, "God leverages pain in powerful and mysterious ways." We'll talk about this in more detail in the next chapter, but it's connected to the idea that the path through pain runs on parallel tracks. On one track is the gut-clawing ache of loss and grief. But on the other track are the joy and peace from God. On that track, there is also evidence of his heart and his hand at work in our lives.

In all my study of the world religions and worldviews, Christianity is the only one that makes sense of evil and suffering. The Bible is the only book that offers humanity an answer for how to deal with evil and suffering. And the answer is the redemption, reconciliation, and restoration God offers us through Jesus.

I still grieve my daughter's death daily, but I've seen God leverage our tragedy in powerful and mysterious ways. In fact, I would never have had this conversation with Bart had it not been for LeeBeth.

I wish I could say Bart fell to his knees in that parking lot and had a righteous epiphany that altered his faith forever. But that's not what happened. At the very least, verbalizing my response to Bart's questions strengthened my faith. And I pray that your faith will be strengthened too.

What's in Your Box?

I (Ed) grew up listening to all sorts of music, but since LeeBeth's passing, I've had a hunger for Christian music like never before. I've wondered why, and I've concluded that it has to be heaven calling out to me. When we worship, we enter the presence of God. We're at his throne. I know worship is about God, but I also know LeeBeth is right there in heaven worshiping too.

While working out one morning, I was listening to a favorite song called "Revelation Song." I love the way Kari Jobe performs it. To make working out convenient, I have dumbbells in our garage, though I sometimes have to move storage items around to make enough space. So I was listening to my favorite song and doing some triceps extensions when I glanced to the left and noticed a couple of boxes. I thought, "That's odd. I've never seen those boxes before. What has Lisa put in here now?"

Then I saw it, written on the side of the box in magic marker: LeeBeth's china. I started crying while working out, thinking, "For the most part, LeeBeth lived a dynamic life, and here's all we have left of her. Boxes." I walked over and opened one of the boxes that had more in it than just china. Here's what I found.

It's a painting I did for LeeBeth when she was going through a very difficult time at a rehab clinic on South Padre Island. It pictures a boat I named *Grace*.

When I saw it, it made me wonder, "What will be in my box after I'm gone?" If everything my life is about is going to end up in a box, what do I want to leave behind? A box filled with odds and ends? Golf clubs? Sports memorabilia? Trophies? Or do I want a box overflowing with evidence of God's goodness, mementos of a life led by him?

I want to ask you the same question: What will be in your box after you're gone? I pray that when your time on earth draws to a close, your box, like LeeBeth's, will be full of God's amazing grace. We can't earn his grace, but we can receive it even though we don't deserve it. He freely gives his grace to those who trust in him. It flows out of his goodness and his unending love for you and me.

Maybe you've hesitated to take God's hand daily because you don't fully understand his thoughts or his ways. But you don't have to understand God to trust that he is good and has a path through the pain for you. Take his hand daily and he will show you how to take one step at a time, one day at a time, in his grace.

Take a Step

FOUR STEPS ON THE PATH THROUGH PAIN

1. Admit you cannot process pain on your own.

2. Believe Jesus is your loving Lord and anchor.

3. *Choose him daily to lead you by the hand.*

4. Discover hope and healing in community.

- Prior to reading Bart's story, what would your response have been to his question, "Why do bad things happen to good people?" Has your response changed? If so, how?

- Which of the four statements I made to Bart surprised you most? Why?

    1) *We live in a fallen world: our world is not perfect, and we are not good.*

    2) *This is not all there is: this life is not the final chapter for any of us.*

    3) *The worst thing happened to the best person: Jesus suffered the worst pain on our behalf.*

    4) *God leverages pain in powerful and mysterious ways: God offers us his amazing grace.*

- Look at each of the four statements I made to Bart. Go to paththroughpain.com to find additional Bible verses that support each of these responses. Write those passages down in a notebook or in the following space.

CHAPTER 7

Unchecked Baggage

> *Just as a fish can't survive outside*
> *of water, the devil cannot thrive*
> *in an atmosphere of purity in the*
> *center of truth. Truth, holiness,*
> *worship, focus, wisdom, love = the*
> *atmosphere of a Christian's life.*
>
> —Lisa's journal, thirteen weeks
> before LeeBeth's passing

Have you ever been driving on the highway and passed an SUV or van with one of those luggage shells on top? Every time we see one, we think about a family vacation we took years ago when our children were young. The twins were a year old, EJ was three, and LeeBeth was eight. We went to a Hyatt hotel in beautiful San Antonio, Texas, and visited SeaWorld for our summer vacation. Which is a misnomer, by the way. Shortly into parenthood, we found out that it's impossible to take kids on a "vacation." It's a family trip or an outing. Because when the kids are small, the grown-ups need another vacation to recover from family vacation.

We had a Suburban at the time, and with four kids, there was no way all our luggage would fit in the car. So we piled our bags and gear on top of what was already a massive SUV. We had cheap luggage carriers, and getting all the paraphernalia on top of the car was like a CrossFit workout. The trip was in August, in triple-digit heat, and I (Ed) had to take two showers after I packed the car.

When we pulled up to the hotel, the bellhop just stood there. He said, "I've been doing this for eight years, and I've never seen this much luggage from one family on one car." The man looked genuinely nervous and was in no rush to help me dismantle our mountain of baggage.

That was the start of our "vacation."

The vacation itself was great. We had some conflict because everyone was in close quarters, but it was fun. And by the time we checked out, we were all looking forward to getting home. I got up early and went through the same drill of packing the car and loading up all the baggage. I mean, we had portable playpens and strollers and Power Rangers duffel bags—we had it all. I packed it up, and we headed back to Dallas.

When we turned into our neighborhood, I whispered, "Hallelujah!" I may have also added, "I will never, *ever* do that again." As I swung into our driveway on two wheels, I instinctively pushed the garage door opener. And in my excitement, in my elation to be back home, I forgot about the baggage on top of the car. Any guesses what happened next?

I pressed the gas pedal and—*boom!*—it was like a

scene from a movie. Drywall, boards, and nails went flying everywhere. In my rush to be home, I tore that garage to smithereens, and it wasn't a quick or inexpensive fix.

A lot of us might admit that we identify with that story on a personal level. We'd say, "Yeah, I've got some baggage, and it's done some damage." Everybody's got baggage. And the older we get, the more baggage we tend to have. I can testify to that. But when it comes to personal baggage, what are we really talking about? What *is* baggage?

Baggage and Dysfunction

Baggage is our collection of negative experiences. Our trauma. Our wounds. Our unforgiveness. Our heartache. *Baggage* is another word for our unaddressed aggregate pain. Yet we're sort of used to it. We think it's normal. This is how everyone lives, right? But if we stopped and looked around, we'd see the damage our untreated pain is causing. We'd also discover that repairing the damage is costly. And if we keep on living the way we've been living, if we keep on forgetting about the baggage, we'll also keep on damaging relationships and missing opportunities. It will cost us more than we are willing or able to pay.

But time and time again, what do we do? We say, "I'm in control. I'm going to white-knuckle grip the steering wheel of my life and do what I want because I know best. I know best how to function as a parent. I know best how to function as a spouse. I know best how to function as a student. I know best how to function as a single adult."

Really? This delusion that we know what's best for us is part of why we're all dysfunctional. That's why we often use those two words—*baggage* and *dysfunction*—together. Because one inevitably leads to the other. Is it any wonder we're surrounded by a lot of both? That's because we have dissed God's function in our lives. We have said with our words and our actions that we know better than God when it comes to our pain.

It's common for people to say, "Oh yeah, everybody's dysfunctional." And technically, that's true—we are all dysfunctional. But do you come from a dysfunctional family? That's an important question. Because if you do, you've got some baggage. You've got some pain. And if it hasn't been addressed, it's costing you something emotionally, psychologically, and spiritually.

Most of us would very much like to move beyond pain and dysfunction to healing and wholeness. The problem is that we've tried and failed. We don't know how to manage pain God's way. We've prayed the prayers and waited the time, but our pain persists. Our dysfunction grows. The carnage accumulates all around us. That's because a few things still stand in the way of our healing. We've tried to force our way past our pain, but we can't. We're stuck.

Stuck

One morning, my friend and I (Ed) launched a boat out onto a beautiful, dark lake. The water was coffee-black, and lily pads and moss floated on the surface. As we motored across the water, we noticed some crazy creatures on the banks—water moccasins, nutria, alligators, and snapping turtles. We were so distracted by looking at everything on the shore that we missed a hazard right in front of us. *Wham!* We hit something beneath the boat. In a swampy body of water, hitting something is not uncommon, but this something felt substantial.

"We'll keep going," I thought. But we didn't. When I looked around the boat, I saw nothing but the seemingly bottomless muck that surrounded us. We rocked the vessel back and forth, but nothing happened. We paddled, but nothing happened. We cranked up the motor, but nothing happened.

"Oh no," I thought. And I probably said this part out loud: "We're *really* stuck!"

Outwardly, I acted like it was no big deal. But inwardly, I shuddered because I knew what I had to do next. I curled my toes over the transom of the boat and jumped in. I swam beneath the hull, feeling around with my hands for what was messing with us, which was slightly terrifying. What if it was a massive alligator? But I had to keep going; I had to figure out why we were stuck if we wanted to get *un*stuck.

Finally, my hand brushed against something solid with a rough exterior. Bubbles floated to the surface as I groaned. Our problem was big. Massive, actually. It was a big ol' tree stump that had literally impaled our boat—we were a floating shish kebab. The stump had penetrated the boat's fiberglass exterior through to the Styrofoam insulation, so the more we rocked the boat, the more we bored a deep hole into the hull. If we had continued rocking the boat, we would have sunk.

It was a harrowing experience, but also a vivid analogy of what it's like when we get stuck in the dark and murky waters of pain. We do what we can to free ourselves, but we're not getting anywhere. Something beneath the surface keeps us from moving forward. We've hit a stump. And while a stump might take any number of forms in our lives, one stump often underlies them all—the stump of pride.

Consequences of Our Own Sin

While much of the emotional turmoil and hurt we experience comes from painful circumstances that happened *to* us, sometimes our pain is caused *by* us. We suffer because of decisions we've made. It takes courage to admit that and to own our regrettable behavior and poor choices. Even if our decisions were understandable at the time, that doesn't make them acceptable. But no matter what we've done, we can rely on this promise: "If we confess our sins, he is faithful and just and will forgive us our sins and purify us from all unrighteousness" (1 John 1:9 NIV).

If your pain is a result of your own decisions, know that your suffering is not punishment from God. It is simply the natural consequence of going your own way. God forgives you. But, like a good parent, he loves you enough to allow you to experience the consequences of your decisions. This is how all of us learn and grow.

Pride

Pride impales our lives and keeps us stuck in our pain because pride requires denial. Regardless of how much pain we're in, pride says, "I'm fine. I can handle it. I know what I'm doing." And the Bible makes it clear that there are consequences for living this way: "Pride goes before destruction, a haughty spirit before a fall" (Proverbs 16:18 NIV). That's why Lisa and I believe pride is the point of origination and the precursor of all sin.

Think about it. I can't be greedy unless I'm first prideful. I first have to say, "God, what I do with money is my own deal. It's not yours, God. I've worked for it. I've earned it. So I'm going to do what I want with my finances." And just as pride is the precursor to greed, it's the precursor to a host of other things as well. I can't lust unless I think I'm entitled to whatever I want. I can't steal unless I first think I deserve more than I have. I can't lie unless I think my way is justified. And so on.

At the center of all sinful behavior is a focus on *me, me, me*. And when it comes to ending up stuck in our pain, pride impales us by getting us to buy into two lies: "I'm not the problem" and "I don't deserve this." First let us say we are not talking about acts that are illegal, immoral, or unjust that may have happened to you. That is not your fault, and it breaks God's heart. Based on God's standard of righteousness, goodness, and justice those types of things should not happen, but they do because of the evil in the world.

However, what we are talking about, is when we look at the pain or the bad that has happened to us, and we determine for ourselves that we should not have to experience that pain based on our goodness. That's when we have drifted into pride. This becomes especially true as we make comparisons to others and determine these things may happen to them but shouldn't happen to us. Or why would this happen to me and not someone like them. That's specifically the pride we're talking about. When we say something like, "I don't deserve this—I'm so much better than other people who do not have to deal with what I am going through."

LIE 1: "I'M NOT THE PROBLEM"

It's easy to spot pride in others but far more difficult to recognize it in ourselves. When we encounter dysfunction in our relationships, our knee-jerk response is, "I'm not the problem—they are."

Years ago, we lived in a neighborhood where the homes were so pretty. I (Lisa) loved the architecture and the landscaping. The houses had actual yards—something you can't find everywhere these days. But there was one home that stood out, and not in a good way. We didn't know the homeowners, but Ed would sometimes refer to them as Jim and Jill Junkster. I didn't necessarily approve of the moniker, but I couldn't argue with its accuracy. There was *a lot* going on in their yard and driveway.

"We should just go knock on their door," Ed said. "We should ask them if they even notice how much junk they have. It looks like a flea market over there!"

"If you do that, you'd better make sure our yard and house look *immaculate* before you go," I said. "Before you ask those homeowners to clean up their act, we have to make sure *our* act is cleaned up."

When it comes to recognizing the need to deal with baggage and dysfunction, it's tempting to think first about your spouse, your parents, your ex, your boss, your coworker, your teammate, or anyone else in your life. But the Bible tells us we must first consider ourselves. It was Jesus who said, "First get rid of the log in your own eye; then you will see well enough to deal with the speck in your friend's eye" (Matthew 7:5 NLT).

There's no gentle way to say this, so I'll be blunt—if you are the common denominator in all your problems, *you* may be the problem. Often we stay stuck because we're so busy shifting blame in the direction of others that we don't take stock of our own role in our circumstances.

LIE 2: "I DON'T DESERVE THIS"

One of the most difficult forms of pride to recognize is one that might surprise you—it's the pride we take in our goodness. I (Lisa) have had these moments myself. I've experienced pain and thought, "God, I've been good. I've led a moral life. I don't deserve this pain." But rehearsing our own goodness is just another form of pride.

When we're in pain that we don't believe we deserve because of how good we are, pride often whispers, "No one understands your pain. No one gets what you're going through." But that's not the case. The author of Hebrews

127

wrote, "We do not have a high priest who is unable to empathize with our weaknesses, but we have one who has been tempted in every way, just as we are—yet he did not sin. Let us then approach God's throne of grace with confidence, so that we may receive mercy and find grace to help us in our time of need" (Hebrews 4:15–16 NIV).

This passage in Hebrews is talking about Jesus, and he deeply understands your pain because he suffered unimaginable pain himself. Three days before he was crucified, Jesus endured an evening full of emotional whiplash—a night from hell itself. Knowing he was about to die, he wanted to have a meaningful dinner with his best friends, but their conversation devolved into an argument about which among them would be the greatest. When Jesus felt overcome with anguish in the garden of Gethsemane and asked his disciples to pray for him, they fell asleep instead. Then Judas, one of his own, betrayed him. Later, Peter, another of his own, denied him—not once, not twice, but three times. And don't forget the part where Jesus was mocked, tortured, nailed to a cross, and murdered for crimes he didn't commit. When Jesus faced the most excruciating trial of his life, he faced it alone.

In terms of sinlessness, Jesus is the only person to walk the earth who could truly have said, "I don't deserve this," and "No one understands what I'm going through." But he didn't. Instead, he humbled himself and prayed, "Father, if you are willing, please take this cup of suffering away from me. Yet I want your will to be done, not mine" (Luke 22:42 NLT). That's a prayer we can pray as well. Instead of lamenting that no one understands what we're going through, we can humbly ask for mercy and grace in our time of need. Jesus understands.

If pride is keeping you stuck in pain, remove that stump from your life before it sinks your ship.

What's in Your Bag?

Once we recognize how pride might be keeping us stuck, it's time to take a closer look at our unchecked baggage—specifically, the patterns of thought and behavior that repeatedly cause us pain. As we stated earlier you may have experienced great pain that was unjustly perpetrated against you. For many this pain began even when you were a child, and the deep wounds are easily triggered today. God did not cause this pain and there will never be a sufficient answer as to why it happened. But you do need to take the steps and work through your pain, or you are choosing to let it control you. We want to empower you to make the choice to walk your path through pain. We believe in you—you are worth it, so let's work it. Jesus is with you and will help you, but healing cannot really begin until we learn to put our baggage down. That's when we change the ways we think and act that are masking the source of our pain.

It starts when we identify the ways our pain manifests itself, so we can trace it back to its source. It's something like what doctors do to diagnose physical pain. One of the first things they ask is, "What are your symptoms?" In other words, what hurts? What aches? What's bothering you? What brought you here today? Then they work back from the symptoms to identify the source of the pain.

We can take a similar approach with our pain. The symptoms of unchecked emotional baggage might take any number of forms, from approval seeking and anxiety to anger and unforgiveness. To help you name what your baggage might be, we've identified some of the most common dysfunctional patterns people fall into when they're stuck in pain. As you read through the list, consider which ones you resonate with most.

PERFECTIONISM

Some of us manage our pain with perfectionism. This is especially true for those of us who grew up in dysfunctional families. Because of past trauma, we want everything to be right. We are determined not to be messed up like our family was. Nope, we're going to be the opposite. We're going to be perfect.

Or, in what might seem like an ironic twist, perfectionism can also express itself as a determination to live above it all. We decide, "I'm going to be laid back. Nothing's going to bother me. I'm chill." It's still perfectionism because we have to work hard at trying not to work hard. We're perfectionistic in our determination to be laid back, regardless of what it costs us.

Whatever form it takes, perfectionism causes us pain because it leaves no room for grace, no room for God. It's performance based and shame driven.

NEED FOR CONTROL

Ever find yourself thinking thoughts like these? "Why did she choose that? What did he do it that way? If everybody would just do what I told them to do, the world would run a lot smoother."

If any of this sounds familiar, you could be carrying around more pain than you realize. At some point, you may have felt helpless and vulnerable, and now you manage your fear that it could happen again by trying to control everything and everyone around you.

Despite our best efforts, none of us can ever fully control our circumstances or other people. Having control issues in your baggage will compound your pain and regret.

GUILT

Guilt is a big one, isn't it? True guilt is what we feel when we're responsible for wrongdoing; false guilt is what we feel when we take responsibility for something over which we have no control. For example, a child feels guilty when her parents have an argument about how she's performing in school; if she had gotten better grades, they wouldn't have fought. Or parents feel guilty for a child's drug abuse, reasoning that it wouldn't have happened if they'd been better parents. Both are examples of false guilt in action, and some of us are stuck in a pattern of believing that anything that goes wrong is somehow our fault. It might be something we learned in childhood or a coping strategy we developed as an adult, but the result is the same—we're lugging around bags of guilt we weren't meant to carry. We know Jesus says, "Bring it to me," but we don't know how, or we don't feel worthy. So we stay stuck in pain.

EGOTISM

"It's all about me." Egotism is a lot like pride in the sense that we're often blind to it. It's easy to see other people who have an inflated view of their own importance, but it's harder to see the same dynamic in ourselves.

If your baggage is egotism, you may be compensating for low self-esteem and insecurities. To prop up a negative self-image, you need to be the center of attention and feel superior to everyone else. You want everything to revolve around you and believe you should have the final say. And if you're unhappy, you want everybody else to be unhappy too.

That's how egotism deals with the pain of insecurity. And if that's what's in your baggage, it's causing you and the people you love a lot of pain.

CRITICISM

Critical people rarely recognize themselves as critical. Most often, critical people think they're being helpful. That speck of dust isn't going to point itself out, is it? Let's do a quick test. When you listen to a sermon or message or read a book, do you find yourself open to the helpful and convicting parts? Or do you make a mental list of everything you disagree with or the ways you would have said things better? If the latter, you may be using criticism to avoid confronting difficult truths about life or about yourself.

DECEPTION

Maybe you grew up in a household where your parents routinely lied to each other, and you thought that must be normal. Perhaps people you respected and admired got ahead by lying, so you concluded that's what it takes to be successful. Maybe as a kid, you had to lie to get approval from a critical parent or to gain acceptance from friends. Whatever the reason, now you, too, have fallen into a pattern of deceiving, exaggerating, or hiding to cover your tracks.

Deception causes us so much pain, but we're afraid to stop being deceptive because then we'd be exposed. Deception in your baggage will always lead to more deception, more weight to lug around.

ANXIETY

Many of us, including children, teens, and young adults, battle racing thoughts, tension, worry, and generalized fear. Anxiety becomes baggage when we refuse to confront our past and continue in the same patterns that either exacerbate or avoid our anxiety triggers. The causes of anxiety can be multifaceted and complex, but may include past abuse or trauma, current difficulties and stressors, or fear of the future. At its worst, anxiety can be debilitating. Often anxiety is a result of untreated pain, of wounds we're afraid of experiencing again or exposing to others. It can hold us back and limit our purpose. It can even cause physical pain. We don't have to live in anxiety, but many of us do, and we remain in pain as a result.

ANGER

Anger is what we feel when we believe we have been wronged. We might experience anger when we feel attacked, frustrated, or helpless. However, for some, anger becomes a go-to coping mechanism, a way to feel powerful by avoiding vulnerable emotions such as grief, fear, or sadness. We're ready to pounce if someone so much as disagrees with how we take our coffee. Cut us off in traffic? You're taking your life into your hands. Or we may bottle up our anger so we can release it on "special occasions" for maximum impact. That's when we spew all over everyone like a shaken can of toxic soda.

Angry people are in-pain people. But like many other things we've packed in our baggage, anger from pain just perpetuates more pain.

PROMISCUITY

Sexual sin is a sin against ourselves, against the temples of God in which our souls live. Many people who struggle with promiscuity are repeating patterns they saw or experienced growing up. Their parents or siblings had certain behaviors and attitudes toward sex, so they do as well.

Maybe you had an absent father or mother, and sex became the substitute for the love and intimacy you craved. Maybe the only "good" attention you've received has been directed to your body or your sexuality. Perhaps an adult or an older kid violated you in the worst way possible, and sexual acting out became your coping strategy. If you were sexually abused, our hearts break for you. That was not God's will for your life. You didn't deserve to be taken advantage of.

Or maybe you grew up thinking promiscuity was the norm because our culture promotes and even rewards it. That, combined with a need for love and intimacy, set you up for a promiscuous lifestyle that has caused you a great deal of pain.

Whatever the cause, chances are that promiscuity has led you not to the love and intimacy you crave but to self-hatred. You are in pain and don't understand why.

APPROVAL SEEKING

When we grow up hearing mostly negative messages about ourselves at home, at school, on social media, and in culture, we learn that we have to earn approval. That we have to look a certain way to be accepted. That we have to display masculinity, femininity, or sexual appeal to receive approval. That we have to follow certain steps in a certain order to be successful in life. When we can't look that way or feel that way and life doesn't go that way, we feel insecure. And so we seek approval in other places, the wrong places, because we didn't get it from the places we wanted to.

UNFORGIVENESS

Some of us carry around so much guilt and shame in our baggage that we can't figure out how to forgive ourselves. Others of us are weighed down because we are unwilling or unable to forgive others.

Of all the baggage items we've covered, perhaps nothing has the potential to wreck our lives more than remaining stuck in unforgiveness. In part, that's because unpacking the pain of every other item on the list requires forgiveness—we must forgive either ourselves or others to move on. For that reason, we want to spend a little more time unpacking this one.

I (Ed) got a vivid picture of what it looks like to live with the baggage of unforgiveness one day when I was filling up my car at a convenience store gas station. A man walked up to the store with his Doberman pinscher, and before going inside to buy a drink, he leashed the dog to a bench that was anchored in concrete. When something suddenly startled the Doberman, the dog took off on a mad dash toward the busy freeway nearby. He launched with such force, with such torque, that he ripped the bench right out of the concrete!

As the dog ran into the intersection dragging the bench behind him, cars, trucks, and SUVs all screeched to a stop. Although he was able to change directions on a dime to avoid being hit, the bench didn't have his reaction time. It kept heading in the same direction until it slammed into the side of an SUV. *Bam!* When the dog jolted in the other direction, the bench went barreling behind him. *Bam!* It slammed into another car and then another. Car parts were flying everywhere! I stood there in shock. When the owner saw what was happening, he ran out of the store, caught up with the dog, and unleashed it from the bench. Thankfully, no animals or humans were injured.

Now imagine that you're the dog and unforgiveness is the bench. It's not hard to see how dangerous this whole situation is, right? The question is, Who's sitting on your bench?

Who is it you're unable or unwilling to forgive? Yourself? Others? Aside from the original source of pain, what's the collateral damage you're suffering or inflicting on others by dragging unforgiveness around? How has it impacted your relationships, including how you relate to yourself?

If we want to take healthy steps forward on the path through pain, we can't stay leashed to unforgiveness. Don't allow a past hurt or failure to damage your life today or your potential tomorrow. Unleash unforgiveness, release yourself or the other person over to God, and begin living your life without carrying all that weight behind you. Forgiving someone does not mean that what they did to you was okay. Forgiving them does not mean you must trust that person or allow them to be in your life. Forgiving is the ongoing process of releasing that person and that situation to God as you work the steps to process the pain they caused.

The Bible tells us that we should live in a state of forgiveness. But that doesn't mean unleashing unforgiveness happens instantly. Forgiveness is a process, one that can feel unnatural at first. And sometimes we need to forgive more than once as we are hit by new waves of pain from the past. God wants to unleash us from unforgiveness, and with his help, we can learn to forgive. Let us show you how with a process we call 4D forgiveness.

4D Forgiveness

We've found that creating a process and plan helps guide and remind us to do things we don't really want to do. For example, we each have our own chores around the house. We schedule our workouts. We have a process for how we pay bills. We've learned that a certain amount of automation takes the sting out of otherwise painful tasks, forgiveness being one of them.

Forgiveness—of yourself or of others—isn't easy. That's not breaking news. But forgiveness *is* biblical, and it *is* necessary to move forward on the path through pain. The 4D forgiveness process is something Lisa and I have developed over time, and it breaks forgiveness down into manageable steps: defer to God, decide to take initiative, disengage from your emotions, and deliver your enemy to God. How long does this process take? That's up to you. But we'd encourage you to take the first step today. If you can do that, you're one step closer to healing and wholeness.

DEFER TO GOD

Begin by surrendering your unforgiveness to God. You might pray, "God, this whole forgiveness thing is from you. It's a God thing. I've been greatly forgiven. And because I've been greatly forgiven, I want to greatly forgive others and be released from those who have hurt me." And you can admit, "I don't feel it! I don't want to do it! But I know forgiveness is who you are. God, help me to forgive."

If the person you need to forgive is yourself, you might pray, "God, I don't feel worthy of your forgiveness. I don't even feel worthy of my own! But I know that to heal, I have to release myself from the bondage of unforgiveness, even unforgiveness toward myself. To do that, I need your help. I repent of my sin and ask that you help me view myself the way you do—as wholly blameless and wholly forgiven."

DECIDE TO TAKE THE INITIATIVE

God gives us the opportunity to choose forgiveness, but we have to follow through on it. It's our call. The apostle Paul underscored this when he wrote, "If it is possible, *as far as it depends on you*, live at peace with everyone" (Romans 12:18 NIV, emphasis added). As far as it depends on who? *You.* Live at peace with everyone. It's your choice.

The apostle Paul also wrote, "Be kind and compassionate to one another, forgiving each other" (Ephesians 4:32 NIV). Note that the verb "forgiving" is in the present tense, meaning it is a continual, ongoing act. We continually forgive, just as God has forgiven us. Don't wait for the other person to own up or apologize; that may never happen. Take the initiative.

DISENGAGE FROM YOUR EMOTIONS

None of us likes forgiving people who hurt us. We don't like them. We're mad at them. We don't want to do it. But if we wait until we feel like it, we'll never forgive. It's also true that if we don't feel like forgiving, that's probably a good indicator that we do need to forgive.

Through the prophet Isaiah, God says, "I, even I, am he who blots out your transgressions . . . and remembers your sins no more" (Isaiah 43:25 NIV). That doesn't mean God gives himself amnesia, that he suddenly just forgets. No, God chooses not to remember our sins, to not hold them against us. The miracle of forgiveness happens not in forgetting what happened but in choosing to forgive what happened. Because when we choose to forgive, our memories can become memorials to the grace of God. And the more we make those memorials, the sooner we won't think so much about what happened. That, in turn, continues to free us up to be the person God created us to be.

DELIVER YOUR ENEMY TO GOD

Jesus taught us that we are to pray for our enemies, but left to ourselves, those prayers would probably sound something like this: "God, show mercy to me but justice to them. Go get 'em, God!" But here's how Jesus put it: "Love your enemies, do good to those who hate you, bless those who curse you, pray for those who mistreat you" (Luke 6:27–28 NIV).

That changes the whole vibe about how we view our enemies, doesn't it? Loving our enemies doesn't mean excusing what they've done or acting like the hurt they caused didn't happen. But we're to pray for them and give them to God. We let God settle the score. We don't have to worry about it. Delivering your enemy to God is a huge step of faith, but a great peace comes with it.

The healing impact of forgiveness is reflected in our lives emotionally, relationally, and sometimes even physically. But even more important, our spiritual health and relationship with God vastly improve when we unleash ourselves from unforgiveness.

In his grace and mercy, God has forgiven us of every wrong we have ever done. He has removed our sins from us "as far as the east is from the west" (Psalm 103:12 NIV). And because he has granted us his forgiveness, he calls us to extend that same grace and forgiveness to others. When we finally let go of the bitterness or hate, we are unleashed from the baggage that has caused so much pain in our lives and freed up to move forward on the path through pain.

Let's Check Our Baggage

If you're lugging around a lot of painful baggage, you're far from alone. We've all got baggage, our collection of untreated pain. And at some point, we've all slung our bags around, leaving a trail of carnage in our wake. Many of us don't realize how much our untreated pain is costing us. We may or may not have been taught any better, but we often feel like we don't know what to do next. But here is one thing you can do. Stop for a moment right now, right where you are, and acknowledge your baggage. Whatever it may be, invite God to help you unzip it, open it up, and see what's inside.

You might be surprised by how much of the pain in your life originates in your own unchecked baggage. But be greatly encouraged that you don't have to live with baggage. The beauty of a growing relationship with Jesus is his offer to shoulder the load for us. And it can be accomplished with Step 3—choosing him daily to lead you by the hand. He invites us to come to him, all who are weary and burdened, and to exchange our baggage for his—for rest (Matthew 11:28). That's a trade we won't pass up! And we hope you don't either.

Take a Step

FOUR STEPS ON THE PATH THROUGH PAIN

1. *Admit you cannot process pain on your own.*

2. Believe Jesus is your loving Lord and anchor.

3. *Choose him daily to lead you by the hand.*

4. Discover hope and healing in community.

- Of the patterns of thought and behavior that repeatedly cause us pain, which do you recognize most in your own life? What core belief is at the center of that pattern? How can you stop the cycle and break the pattern today?

- What carnage has been left in the pathway of your baggage? Think about relationships, jobs, and opportunities. Has the price of your baggage become too much to bear? Are you willing to accept Jesus's invitation to trade your baggage for rest?

- Write down a list of all the unwanted "items" in your baggage: failed relationships, hurtful situations, wounds, and sources of pain. Then put them in order, first listing the "item" that feels heaviest. For the next twenty-four hours, whenever you think of this item, pray, "God, I exchange my baggage for yours."

CHAPTER 8

You-Turn

*Thank you, Jesus, that you don't
waste our pain.*

—Lisa's journal, one month
after LeeBeth's passing

At ninety-four years old, my (Lisa's) mom went to heaven just before Thanksgiving 2022. The arrangements were made, and we flew to Columbia, South Carolina, for her life celebration. It was indeed a celebration because Mom had lived a beautiful life for Jesus, and she was now in his presence.

After the funeral service, as we headed back to the airport to catch our flight, we made the executive decision to go to Hudson's, one of Columbia's best barbecue spots. If you haven't had South Carolina's mustard-based pork barbecue, then have you ever had real barbecue? I don't think so.

Ed, as he has already admitted, is directionally

challenged. So the first thing we did was put Hudson's address into the map app on Ed's phone so we could let Siri lead the way. And bless Siri's robotic heart, she announced we were just thirty minutes from our destination. So I sat back in my seat, happy to be free from my navigational duties because Siri was on the job.

As we drove, I was checking emails on my phone and trying to get a few things done so I could fully engage with my family at the restaurant. Then I heard Siri say, "Exit now." But we did not exit. Ed didn't even tap the brakes. From the back seat, our son, EJ, said, "Uh, Dad? You just missed the exit."

"I know, I know," Ed said. "If Siri would just speak up a little sooner!"

So we had to make a U-turn. Only, in this part of South Carolina, the exits are far apart. It was several miles and another ten minutes before we were able to turn around, which left us once again thirty minutes away from Hudson's. We were no closer than when we started!

U-turns are never easy, but we've all had to make them. Not only on the highways we travel but in the lives we live. I know I have. I've been driving down the highway of life thinking I'm on the right track when the gentle voice of the Holy Spirit speaks, but I ignore him. Then—*bam!*—I'm heading in the wrong direction. I've gotten distracted or been too focused on my own plans and missed the voice of God. When this happens, God forgives you. But, like a good parent, he loves you enough to allow you to experience the consequences of your decisions. This is how all of us learn and grow.

When LeeBeth was dealing with her addiction, we had to make the tough decision to put her in a rehab facility. Because she was an adult, she had to consent to go, and we were grateful when she agreed this was best for her. But once she was there, she hated it and questioned why we would ever make her go there. She viewed the staff and rehab team as enemies and repeatedly told us we were wasting our money. To do a you-turn, she was going to have to deal with the consequences of her behavior. It was a necessary step toward healing, but it didn't feel good.

Because we are all sinful human beings, we're guessing you can probably relate to this dynamic. You want to make a change, you want to experience healing, but you don't want to go through the pain it requires. And yet if you want to travel this path through pain that God has laid out for you, there's no shortcut. You need to make a you-turn.

What do we mean by you-turn? We mean taking your own sin seriously. It's not a topic most of us like to talk about, but Jesus talked about it quite a bit. A you-turn is repentance. When you're going in one direction and you make the choice to stop, turn around, and go the opposite direction, that's repentance. Repentance is a change of mind that results in a change of direction. It's a you-turn.

Repentance Is the Necessary You-Turn

When you hear the word *repentance*, what first comes to mind? How do you respond? Do you recoil? Feel dread or guilt? Think about some guy standing on the street corner wearing a sandwich board that says, "Repent or burn in hell!"? Imagine a pastor slamming his fist on the pulpit, demanding, "Repent! Repent! Repent!"?

Think about it. When was the last time you spent any time pondering or studying the topic of repentance? If it has been a while, as it probably has been for most of us, then we've got good news. Repentance doesn't set us up for condemnation; it positions us for forgiveness. Not until we turn from our sin are we ready to fall into the arms of our forgiving Father.

The problem most of us have with repentance is that it feels disconnected from grace. We hurry to skip over repentance so we can move toward forgiveness, love, mercy, and tears of joy. But that's a problem because repentance must come first before we can truly experience those good things.

Repentance doesn't have to be shaming—in fact, it shouldn't be! Paul tells us that there is no condemnation for those who belong to Jesus (Romans 8:1). Instead of avoiding repentance, we should run to it! Repentance offers us freedom and wholeness, neither of which we can receive any other way. If I haven't convinced you of the value of repentance yet, here are four reasons we should always be ready to repent: Repentance is "brutiful," repentance is commanded, repentance is more than an apology, and repentance leads to healing.

REPENTANCE IS BRUTIFUL

There's a perfect word to describe our path through pain. It's also a good word to describe the process of repentance: *brutiful*. Repentance is both brutal and beautiful. Repentance isn't easy; it can actually be painful. This sounds counter-intuitive when we're talking about repentance as a pathway through pain, but that's how it works.

The courage required to make a you-turn, to truly repent, may be why so few pastors speak on it and why so few books are written on it. Sermons and books on grace? Yes. Sermons and books on mercy? Absolutely. Sermons and books on repentance? Not so much. But the word *repentance* and words like it are used over fifty times in the New Testament. We have to talk about repentance, if for no other reason than Jesus himself talked about it.

Often, repentance requires us to walk away from things or people we once loved or still love: maybe an impure relationship, a sinful habit, or even wrong thinking that we used to take comfort in. You can expect a grieving period when you repent, and grieving hurts. But 2 Corinthians 7:10 (NIV) brings us the promise that "godly sorrow brings repentance that leads to salvation and leaves no regret." That's where the beautiful aspect of repentance comes in—salvation and no regrets. I'll take a little brutality when salvation and no regrets are the trade-offs.

REPENTANCE IS COMMANDED

Scripture says, God has overlooked the times when people did not know him, but now he commands all people everywhere to repent (Acts 17:30, paraphrased). *Wow*. That verse alone makes God's position on repentance clear. He's not playing around. He's not treading lightly. God commands repentance.

147

I (Lisa) love to ask clarifying follow-up questions. I like to know more, but I prefer to know *everything*. So when I read that God commands us to repent, my natural reaction is to wonder why. Why is repentance a command? Why does it matter so much to God? Why should it matter to me?

The apostle Paul gives a succinct yet thorough response to those questions: "For sin pays its wage—death" (Romans 6:23 GNT). You may have heard it phrased this way: "For the wages of sin is death." Anytime death is mentioned in Scripture, it has to do with separation. So the price of our sin is death—eternal separation from our heavenly Father.

As soon as LeeBeth's soul left her body, we were separated in ways I never imagined I would experience as her mother. To feel that distance from my child was unnatural. It violated the expected order of my life. And without the hope of heaven—without the guarantee that one day my daughter and I will be reunited—I would not be able to thrive right now. The pain of life, and especially the pain of LeeBeth's death, would have devoured me long ago. That's what separation does. It tears apart what belongs together.

Sin separates us from God, and that separation stings because we were created to be in relationship with him. But when we repent, God heals what was broken and tears down the wall of sin that separates us from him. When we turn from our sin and choose to follow Jesus, we experience salvation. But repentance isn't a one-and-done deal. The process that follows salvation is called *sanctification*. Sanctification means becoming progressively more like Jesus. As we are confronted by our sin through the ups and downs of life, we have opportunities to choose repentance again and again. It's through this process that God refines and transforms us so that we look more like his Son.

This process can be derailed when we focus on sin's consequences rather than sin itself. For example, greed causes financial stress, but instead of repenting of greed, we focus on managing the stress. Jealousy causes relational stress, but instead of repenting of jealousy, we focus on managing the stress. Dishonesty causes career stress, but instead of repenting of dishonesty, we focus on managing the stress. All sin has earthly, human consequences. Have you found that to be true? I have. When I sin and experience the consequences, my attitude is, "These consequences are painful. This hurts. This is uncomfortable. Why can't God change my consequences?"

But that's not what God does. God says, "How did you get into this situation to begin with? What's at the root? What's the cause?" Sin is at the root of a lot of our pain. Like a good healer, God doesn't want to treat only the symptom (pain), he wants us to face the problem (sin). God commands us to repent daily because he wants to heal us. He wants so much more for us than we'd settle for on our own.

REPENTANCE IS MORE THAN AN APOLOGY

While we might struggle with repentance, most of us will apologize when we come face-to-face with our sin. We'll say, "God, I'm sorry." While it's good to apologize, that's not the totality of repentance. I can even feel remorseful and cry, "I'm sorry, I shouldn't have done that." But that's not necessarily repentance.

Many of us have lost sight of what a genuine apology and true repentance are because of the numbing insincerity of faux confessions. We see celebrities, pastors, and politicians make apologies all the time. For example, "I regret my actions and any harm they might have caused." What does that even mean? Most of the time these public displays of remorse are made by people who've been caught. They make a general acknowledgment of fault because they want to avoid their consequences. They don't want to lose their marriage. They don't want to lose their financial security. They don't want to lose their career. So they say a blanket "I'm sorry" as part of a damage containment and public relations strategy.

The apostle Paul tells us the difference between godly contrition and a public relations stunt: **"Godly sorrow brings repentance that leads to salvation and leaves no regret, but worldly sorrow brings death"** (2 Corinthians 7:10 NIV). Worldly sorrow is about me; godly sorrow is about God. Many times, my apologies have been about me. "Okay, God. I've hurt Ed's heart. But you know, he's hurt my heart before too." What I need to understand is that my actions have first broken the heart of God. Confession is a part of repentance. Yes, I must tell the truth about my condition; I must agree with God about a specific sin. But in repentance, I make that you-turn. I choose to go a different direction and change my thinking. Instead, I start with, "God, I know hurting Ed hurt you. I was being petty and short-tempered.

I repent of my words and actions. I don't want to hurt either of you. Please forgive me." And then I receive forgiveness and healing.

Once we have confessed and repented of our sin, then we are ready to walk out our you-turn by being obedient to God, especially when it comes to the areas in which we tend to fail. We do that by putting up guardrails that protect us from veering off-course again. That's part of how we choose God's hand daily and let him lead us in the opposite direction from patterned thoughts and behaviors that lead to more sin and more pain.

REPENTANCE LEADS TO HEALING

If he were alive today, King David's Wikipedia page would describe him as a multibillionaire, poet, musician, and military genius. But despite his gifts and accomplishments, he still succumbed to temptation. On a day when he should have been out on the battlefield with his men, David was instead at home and happened to see a woman named Bathsheba taking a bath (2 Samuel 11).

Bathsheba was beautiful and David lusted after her. It's not the first look that messes you up, it's the second and third look. And David kept looking. He sent someone to find out about her and learned her name and that she was the wife of Uriah the Hittite, who was away at war. But still, David kept looking. Maybe not with his eyes, but with his mind. I imagine he replayed the bath scene over and over. That's where adultery usually starts—in the world of fantasy. But David made his fantasy a reality, eventually getting

Bathsheba pregnant and essentially having her husband murdered.

David had a friend named Nathan who was a prophet. Nathan knew David pretty well, and he was aware of what David had done. Nathan had a conversation with David about a year after the dramatic events unfolded.

David had started out as a shepherd boy. He loved sheep and animals, so Nathan used that knowledge to connect with David during their talk. Nathan basically said, "David, I want to tell you a story. There was a rich guy who had a bunch of beautiful land—just gorgeous. He had the best of the best. He had a purebred this and a purebred that. In the same village was a poor man. He only had one lamb, and this lamb was his pet. He and his kids loved this lamb. He fed the lamb by hand, and it slept in their house. Well, when the rich man had a guest come to stay with him, he said, 'I'm gonna serve some lamb chops for dinner.' But instead of taking one of his own lambs, he took the prized lamb from the poor man. He slaughtered that beloved lamb and served it up to his guest."

David clearly had no idea where Nathan was going with this story, because he was outraged:

> David burned with anger against the man and said to Nathan, "As surely as the LORD lives, the man who did this must die! He must pay for that lamb four times over, because he did such a thing and had no pity."
>
> Then Nathan said to David, "You are the man!"
> (2 Samuel 12:5–7 NIV)

I want to ask you today, friend: Are you that man? Are you that woman? Is there sin in your life that you've yet to confess? Maybe it's time to start your journey toward repentance by saying, "You know what, God? I have excused this anger toward you for too long. I have excused my hatred of this person for too long. I have excused my choices for too long. I have sinned."

Why would you do that? Because a lack of confession and repentance causes pain. Because you want to be healed! David wrote,

> When I refused to confess my sin,
>> my body wasted away,
>> and I groaned all day long.
> Day and night your hand of discipline was
>> heavy on me.
>> My strength evaporated like water in the
>>> summer heat. (Psalm 32:3–4 NLT)

Now consider the contrast after David made a you-turn:

> Finally, I confessed all my sins to you
>> and stopped trying to hide my guilt.
> I said to myself, "I will confess my rebellion to
>> the LORD."
>> And you forgave me! All my guilt is gone.
>> (Psalm 32:5 NLT)

Confession is essential to repentance, repentance is

essential to forgiveness, and forgiveness is the vehicle of healing. Without confession and repentance, there's a barrier between you and God—between you and *healing*. God didn't put it there, you did (Isaiah 59:2). And the only way to break through that barrier is repentance.

Through confession and repentance, God heals our souls and draws us closer to him, providing the opportunity for a deeper and more meaningful connection.

One Family's Story of Pain, Repentance, and Healing

Kelly's wife, Rita, received the devastating news that her treatment wasn't working. After eleven months of courageously battling breast cancer, Rita went home to meet her Savior. Kelly and Rita had been following the Lord together for years, and Kelly wanted to honor Rita by bringing glory to Jesus. At a time when it would have been much easier to retreat and internalize the pain he felt, he focused his energy instead on bringing his family members to church, some of them for the first time.

Trauma had left one of Kelly's daughters, Erica, feeling alone and scared for most of her life. She couldn't shake her anger toward God for what had happened to her. And she was angry about the death of Rita, her stepmother. Kelly and Rita were the most faithful people she had ever known, and she had watched them suffer pain and loss throughout Rita's illness. She was mad at God, and the last place she wanted to be was in a church.

Despite her anger, she decided to give church a chance for Kelly's sake and because her kids had started attending the youth ministry and begged her to come with them. The family had been so warmly received and cared for after Rita's death that they felt the love and hope of God when they were at their lowest. Then Erica's son, Caeden, made the bold decision to commit his life to Christ.

Erica met with one of our Fellowship Church pastors soon after her first visit and decided that she could no longer continue living with so much anger. She decided to change direction, confessing her sin and releasing her pain and shame to Christ. In that moment, she was fully forgiven. Her confession opened the door to repentance. And her repentance enabled her to receive the gift of God's forgiveness.

Erica, her husband, and their four children have now all given their lives to Christ. They have found a home at our church and are on fire for the things of God. They've even begun inviting their friends to experience the same community, acceptance, and healing that they have. The journey ahead will not be easy, but we know God will strengthen this family with the hope that comes only from Christ. As Kelly shared, "We've surrendered our pain to the Lord, and he has used the tragedy of Rita's death to awaken people's souls and pour out immeasurable amounts of grace on my family. Now they are members of his family forever!"

Take Out the Trash

Most of us live with the benefit of a municipal trash pickup, which means we don't think about our trash that much. At least, we don't! It routinely gets picked up once a week, every week. We notice our garbage only when it *doesn't* get taken away for some reason. It smells, becomes an eyesore, and attracts rodents and bugs. It's the same way with sin. If we fail to address it regularly, it piles up. Eventually, it becomes impossible to ignore because our lives stink! That's why we must make it a habit to ask God to search our hearts and reveal places where we need to do a you-turn back to him.

As we work through the process to remove pain from our lives, it is critical to diminish any distance between us and God. And the way to do that is to consistently take out our personal trash as an act of obedience. We're talking not only about sin but also about patterns of thought and behavior that lead to sin.

We're talking about logging onto the internet when you're home alone and it's late at night. You know there's a good chance one thing may lead to another, that you'll end up searching sites that will take you places you don't need to go. We're talking about going to the hotel bar on a business trip for just "one drink to take the edge off." We're talking about getting a "We're having a sale!" email from your favorite store and clicking the link when you know you don't have the money to spend. We're talking about spending time with the friend who always has the latest gossip. We're talking about taking the route home that leads you past the part of town where temptation lies.

On the surface, these acts aren't necessarily sinful, but if they lead you to sin, they belong in the trash. It's time to walk the trash to the curb, put it down, and do a you-turn. And by God's grace let us not go back! You might protest, "But you don't understand me—you don't understand my temptations, my struggles. It's impossible for me." But Paul tells us, "The temptations in your life are no different from what others experience. And God is faithful. He will not allow the temptation to be more than you can stand. When you are tempted, he will show you a way out so that you can endure" (1 Corinthians 10:13 NLT).

That is great news! God is faithful and loyal to you and invites you to be faithful and loyal to him. He is so committed to your healing and growth that he promises to show you a "way out" when you are tempted. There is a God-given way for you to take out the trash. Are you asking him to show you what it is? Do you desire God more than whatever it is that tempts you? Are you ready to make a you-turn?

We all have trash we need to take out. The problem is when we end up living in the equivalent of a trash dump because we've accepted our self-defeating thoughts and habits for so long. They've become part of who we are, part of our identity.

"I'm just that way."

"I'm just an angry person."

"I'm just a loner."

"I'm just a sexual person."

"I'm just an anxious person."

"I'm just a competitive person."

If we want to experience the healing that comes from confession, repentance, and obedience, then we must make a habit of taking out the trash.

Let's say your anger has caused pain for you and the people around you. Instead of saying, "Lord, I get angry. I'm sorry for that. Please forgive me," be specific about how you've sinned and how you are tempted to sin. For example, "Father, I got angry at work yesterday and I'm so sorry. Please forgive me. I need your help today because I'm going to be in a difficult meeting. I know I'll be tempted to be defensive, to one-up people, to be mean-spirited, to get angry. Lord, give me your strength today to respond the way I should."

Or "Lord, I have to be around a coworker tomorrow who causes my competitive nature to rise up. All I feel is envy for the clothes she wears, the car she drives, and the neighborhood where she lives. When I'm with her, please help me to take your hand. I want to choose gratitude instead and trust that I already have everything I need. Keep me from sin." Once you take the trash out to the street, you can take the truth to the streets!

The Truth Will Set You Free

When LeeBeth died, we had a choice: whether or not to tell the truth about what happened. We couldn't confess or repent for LeeBeth, but we could be obedient. Scripture is clear that we must not lie (Exodus 20:16). There's no room for creative interpretation there. There's no wiggle room in that commandment. Even so, we felt protective of LeeBeth and wanted to honor her. There was exponentially more good than bad in and from LeeBeth's life, and we didn't want to diminish that by focusing on the tragic circumstances of her death. But we knew we could not lie about how she died. We couldn't even sugarcoat it with silence. We had to be obedient and transparent.

Our first public statement, written by Ed, conveyed what we had to say:

> It is with great sadness that I write these words. Last night, our precious and cherished daughter LeeBeth passed away. She was our firstborn, and we celebrate her life. LeeBeth was a bright, intelligent, strong, creative, witty, and faithful young woman. We love our daughter, and she loved the Lord. Because of her relationship with Jesus, she is now healed and whole in his presence. We ask that you pray for our family, our church, and so many others who loved LeeBeth deeply.

These are words no parent wants to write, words no parent should ever have to write. We still weren't exactly sure yet how to share LeeBeth's story, but the announcement bought us some time to gather ourselves before we shared more details.

About a month later, on Valentine's Day 2021, we stood before a gathering of our church family and told the truth. We confessed what we could, repented what we could, and were fully obedient to the commandment of God. The response was amazing. People from every corner of the world said, "Thank you." They thanked us for telling the truth, for being real, for being honest. They thanked us for shedding light on a disease that ravages the lives of so many.

Jesus said, "You will know the truth, and the truth will set you free" (John 8:32 NIV). And we have found that when we tell the truth about our pain, God uses it to do the same for others. We've had countless people report taking a you-turn because of our obedience. We've been blessed beyond measure and girded with strength by every story of someone who said, "LeeBeth's passing changed my life. Changed my daughter's life. Changed my friend's life." There is *power* in the pathway through pain. God wants to restore us and set us free, but first we have to be willing to tell the truth about our lives.

The Time Is Now

Do you need to make a you-turn away from the habits and behaviors that are causing pain?

Confession says, "I'm changing my words."

Repentance says, "I'm changing my ways."

Obedience says, "I'm changing my walk."

In chapter 1, we told you about a question we asked LeeBeth just hours before her heartbreaking death. We would like to ask you that question now.

Do you want to live?

We're not just asking if you want to avoid death, we're asking if you want to truly live. Do you want to live a life that isn't dominated by pain? Do you want to leave behind the anger, blame, confusion, depression, emptiness, frustration, guilt, shame, and hopelessness that have defined your life? Do you want to live a life of hope, healing, and wholeness? Do you want to live out the purposes God has for you?

If so, you can start today by praying this prayer:

God, I confess my sin to you: _____. I don't want to just escape the pain; I want to experience your healing. Today, I choose to turn from my sin. Thank you for your forgiveness. Please help me continue to turn to you, moment by moment and day by day, as I walk in obedience to you. I trust you to guide me as I travel on this path through my pain to the purpose you have for me. Today, I choose to live! In Jesus's name. Amen.

The beauty of a you-turn is that you don't have to drive down the highway of life looking for a place to stop and turn around. You can do it right now, at this very moment. Your life can go a completely different direction. And you can find healing and wholeness that you never imagined possible.

Take a Step

FOUR STEPS ON THE PATH THROUGH PAIN

1. Admit you cannot process pain on your own.

2. Believe Jesus is your loving Lord and anchor.

3. ***Choose him daily to lead you by the hand.***

4. Discover hope and healing in community.

- In the past, what has kept you from confession and repentance? How have your views of both changed since reading this chapter?

- Of the four reasons we should always be ready to repent, which gives you the most encouragement?

- Schedule some alone time in the next seventy-two hours to confess and repent. Once you schedule it, don't approach it with dread! Shift your perspective to view this time as an opportunity to remove any barriers that sin has created between you and God.

- Ask God to reveal to you any sin in your life. You might make a list of these things and, one by one, confess them to God and receive his forgiveness. Draw a line through each sin, symbolizing your repentance and turning away from that sin with the help of Jesus.

   Here are some Bible verses to encourage you as you become vulnerable with God:

Search me, God, and know my heart;
    test me and know my anxious thoughts.
See if there is any offensive way in me,
    and lead me in the way everlasting. (Psalm
        139:23–24 NIV)

If we confess our sins, he is faithful and just and will forgive us our sins and purify us from all unrighteousness. (1 John 1:9 NIV)

CHAPTER 9

It's like Tie-Dye

I miss you, LeeBeth, to the core of my being! My heart aches with an excruciating pain. But LeeBeth, you, my precious child, are healed. Heaven has you. Thank you, Jesus, that heaven is your home.

—Lisa's journal, eleven months

after LeeBeth's passing

I (Lisa) loved LeeBeth's sense of style. She always knew what would look good, whether it was dressing a stage set or dressing herself. She looked beautiful in anything. She had such an effortless look. She could elevate a T-shirt, and she could dress down a beaded gown. I always admired her for that. A few years back, she let me know an old trend was making a comeback—tie-dye. As soon as she told me, I started seeing it everywhere in all sorts of colors. And not just in clothes either. In art, bags, even furniture.

The Christmas before LeeBeth passed, just weeks before I got that dreaded call, we celebrated the holiday in matching tie-dye and took what would become our last family photo together. God knew.

Many years ago, for a message series we were doing at our church, LeeBeth suggested we use tie-dye as a visual. She was right—it turned out perfectly. Ed and I made a bunch of tie-dye shirts in our kitchen for the band to wear. If you don't know Ed, he's an artist. He loves creating beautiful things with his hands. He's incredibly talented, but he'd never tell you that. Anyway, we were hanging up the shirts to dry and admiring our handiwork when it struck me. *The pains and struggles we experience in our lives are a lot like tie-dye.*

Tie-dying is a tough process. You knot or bunch the fabric and tie everything in place with rubber bands to create a pattern. Next, you immerse the whole thing in boiling water with dye and let it sit. Then you remove the fabric from the dye, let it cool, and carefully cut away the rubber bands. That's when you finally get to see what you've created. And the beautiful thing is, no two turn out the same.

The tie-dye process reminded me of what we go through in life. We all end up with knots, bunches, twists, and imperfections that mark our lives. And yet, as we deal with those issues, our lives can be colored with a uniquely beautiful pattern. The tie-dye pattern of my life is different from the tie-dye pattern of yours, but the beauty in both comes from what the apostle James described as "trials of many kinds" (James 1:2 NIV).

Count It All Joy

The book of James is all about spiritual development and maturity. James doesn't pull punches; his writing is sometimes what we might call "in your face." But I love the challenge in James's counterintuitive perspective on pain: "Consider it pure joy, my brothers and sisters, whenever you face trials of many kinds" (James 1:2 NIV). Or another translation puts it this way: "*Count* it all joy when you fall into various trials" (NKJV, emphasis added).

Count is a mathematical term. To count something as joy suggests that there's value in examining the attributes and outcomes of our trials and looking for any positive aspects of our pain. In other words, we can look for the silver lining in the black storm clouds of pain. I (Lisa) agree with James, and it is beneficial to look for a silver lining, but let me offer two caveats: (1) resist the temptation to put your silver lining on anyone else's pain process, and (2) don't skim over your pain in a rush to find the silver lining.

Throughout my life, I have tried to do what James taught by quickly looking for the silver lining in difficult situations. But I've learned that Ed and I process pain differently. He needs more time. He first needs to sit or rest in a difficult situation, whether large or small. In the initial stages of his process, he talks about his trial, thinks about it, and verbalizes his emotions. Then he often needs more time to work through things in his mind.

There have been days in our grief journey when I have felt pretty good and Ed has struggled. And there have been days when Ed felt ready to take on the world and I had to fight to hold myself together. Just as each tie-dyed item is unique, the journey each of us takes through pain is unique. Everyone has their own process, which is why it's important not only to process pain in your own way and at your own pace but also to allow others to do the same.

It's also important to work through our pain, which we'll address later in the chapter. We definitely don't want to skim over it, which can happen if we move too quickly to the silver lining. If we rush through the healthy processing of pain, we may end up taking one step forward and two steps back. Sweeping emotions such as anger, hurt, disappointment, or sadness under the rug does us no good. Rather, it can end up prolonging our pain.

Imagine that you are in a painful situation and someone sends you a text that says, "I heard something bad happened today, but you should consider it joy!" How would you feel? If you're anything like me, it probably wouldn't fill you with good feelings. And I'm guessing those who first read James's statement about trials and joy probably had a similar reaction. *What? How am I supposed to consider my suffering pure joy? When I'm in pain, are you saying I should feel happy about it?*

No, not exactly.

James didn't say, "When you encounter trials, be happy about it." He said, "Consider it joy." Remember, happiness and joy are two different things. Happiness comes from the Latin root word *hap*, which means "chance." Happiness is based on happenings. If you're happening or it's happening, you're happy. That's not a bad thing, but it is a shallow thing. James is talking about something much deeper than happiness, which is *joy*. Joy might be best understood as tranquility of the soul. When we're in pain, joy is trusting that God is nevertheless at work on our behalf, even through our trials. While happiness depends on the superficial circumstances of our lives, joy is a spiritual dive to the core of our faith in God.

How do we face trials with a spirit of joy? I think the answer goes back to the word *consider* or *count*. As James uses the word, it means "to evaluate." It's an accounting term. When we choose to see trials through the eyes of faith, we identify them as assets and credit them to our spiritual portfolio. Conversely, when we choose *not* to see our trials through the eyes of faith, we identify them as liabilities and list them as debits. James encourages us to look for the spiritual assets or benefits of our trials and to consider them credits to our faith, which means pain has the potential to benefit us.

The Potential Benefits of Pain

In chapter 3, we touched on what James wrote about trials producing perseverance in our lives (James 1:3), but there are also other ways we can learn to consider our pain an asset rather than a liability. Specifically, pain can motivate us to pray, push us to serve, be a growth opportunity, and remind us to look and listen for pain in the lives of others.

PAIN MOTIVATES US TO PRAY

Even though Ed and I are still traveling this path of pain, we can already see benefits that bring us joy. One benefit is that pain motivates us to pray. When LeeBeth died, we were comforted by the many texts and notes from individuals telling us we were the object of their prayers. We counted on these prayers and treasured them, knowing that God was using an army of his children to help us walk through our tragedy day by day. Although "I'm praying for you" may sound like a cliché, it's no cliché to someone in the throes of a painful storm. We held tightly to those words, counting on them as if our lives depended on them.

Having been on the receiving end of countless prayers, I am now motivated like never before to pray for others experiencing pain. Hurt is all around, near and far, and prayer matters. And I have a whole new perspective on the apostle Paul's admonition to "pray without ceasing" (1 Thessalonians 5:17 NKJV). It doesn't matter where I am or what time it is, it just matters that I pray. I could be in line at the grocery store and pray. I could be driving or stuck in traffic and pray. God might drop a name in my mind, or I might pray when I see someone who appears to be struggling. I believe my motivation to pray without ceasing is a direct result of being on the receiving end of so many prayers during my darkest, most painful season.

Because I have a deeper understanding of the need of prayer, I pray—constantly. I pray for myself and how I'm dealing with pain. I pray for my family and how pain is affecting them. I pray for others experiencing pain. Hospitals are full of people who need prayer. Funeral homes have a steady flow of families who need prayer. Ambulances head to scenes where sick or wounded people need prayer. Our neighborhoods are lined with homes occupied by people who need prayer. The weight of my pain has been lifted through prayer, and I want others to experience that as well.

PAIN PUSHES US TO SERVE

When we were making plans for LeeBeth's celebration of life service, I received a text from my friend Fran. "Hey, girl, Steve and I have a pot of soup we want to drop by the house." It may have been a simple thing, but that pot of soup could just as easily have been a stash of gold nuggets. Fran's text and thoughtful kindness meant the world to me and to our family. You never know what simple thing you might do that will reach deep into the heart of someone in pain. If you think such things don't matter, you're wrong—they matter.

A year later, I was walking with my daughter Laurie through the church when we saw Fran. Laurie told me that she would never forget when Fran brought soup to our home that day. I wasn't even aware Laurie had noticed Fran and Steve dropping it off. The reality is that we don't know how our acts of kindness or simple service will impact someone who is going through pain. Let your pain be a push to serve others in their time of need.

PAIN CAN BE A GROWTH OPPORTUNITY

I (Ed) grew up in the same neighborhood as the Blackstone boys, Rip, Fred, and Lawton. When all of us were almost teenagers, my brothers and I often played football with them. But their mom had a rule that it had to be touch football—no tackling—which was fine with me. Mrs. Blackstone watched every move her boys made, and she was watching us play from the kitchen window one day when Rip went out for a pass and Fred elbowed him. It wasn't that bad, but Rip hit the turf and whimpered a bit. That was all it took for Mrs. Blackstone to fling open the front door and march our way.

"That's all for today," she said. "It's over. Boys, come in. You mean neighborhood kids, go home."

Wow, talk about overprotective. She was treating her almost teenagers like toddlers. I sometimes wonder how the Blackstone boys are doing today. I don't know, but I wonder.

God doesn't treat us like Mrs. Blackstone treated her boys. He is not an overly protective parent. He allows some rough-and-tumble in our lives. Why? So we can grow.

When James wrote about trials producing perseverance, he also said, "Let perseverance finish its work so that you may be mature and complete, not lacking anything" (James 1:4 NIV). In other words, don't give up! Or, if we use the tie-dye analogy, we might say that James is telling us it's worth persevering through the boiling water and knots of life because there will be beauty on the other side. We can say, "This is hard and I don't understand it, but I believe God is going to use it. He is tie-dying me, and I can be beautiful even in my pain."

God is not satisfied with us remaining spiritual toddlers. He wants us to grow and develop so that we will be mature and complete, lacking nothing. The pain we feel isn't meaningless or wasted. It's allowed so that we will not lack anything. God uses our pain for a purpose—to help us grow in our faith.

PAIN REMINDS US TO LOOK AND LISTEN FOR PAIN IN THE LIVES OF OTHERS

When I (Lisa) went to the airport to return to Dallas from South Carolina on the day LeeBeth died, I was surrounded by people who had no idea what I was experiencing. The security officers didn't know. The gate agents didn't know. The flight attendants didn't know. The other passengers didn't know. No one knew I was heading back home to hug my husband after he had spent the last few hours with our dying daughter. No one knew my heart was broken. No one knew that a long and hard-fought battle with addiction had finally taken my daughter's life. How could they?

On the first anniversary of LeeBeth's passing, I went to the store to buy fresh flowers for the gravesite. I picked some of her favorites, a lot of pink ones. My arms were loaded down as I got to the register and handed the flowers to the clerk. He was friendly and jokingly asked, "Are you having a party?" I had to take a second to gain my composure. I didn't want to make him feel bad, so I chose my words carefully. I told him what I was doing, and he said he was sorry for what I was going through. But I told him that for LeeBeth, and our family, it was sort of a party. In that sense, he was right. Because she is in heaven, we could celebrate.

As we walk through our days, we need to remember that we have no idea what other people might be experiencing or the pain they may be processing at that very moment. You may be passing a car headed to the hospital, or the store clerk scanning your groceries may be in the midst of a divorce. Pain is everywhere, and people we encounter every day are living it. Have you ever pondered this? Think about it. You may be the person who can touch their lives with a kind word, an "I'm sorry you are going through this," a smile, or even an offer to help.

When we go through pain, it reminds us to look and listen for the pain in others so they can feel our love and prayers even in the smallest of ways.

Knowing there are benefits to pain doesn't change our circumstances, but it can change the way we experience them. This knowledge also helps us to persevere and hold on to God's hand when we are ready to process our pain.

Processing Pain

Lisa talked earlier about her ability to look for the silver lining in hard situations, and I (Ed) have always admired that about her. But, as she also said, it's important not to skim over or rush the healing process. Even as we persevere and consider our trials through the lens of joy, we also need to be intentional about processing our grief and losses. To help you begin to do that, we encourage you to work through the pain, let the tears fall, share your grief and anxiety with God, and allow God to use your pain for his glory.

WORK THROUGH THE PAIN

It's called "work" because healing requires action. It requires intention. And it requires your participation. There is nothing passive about moving forward on the path through pain. If you're not sure where to start, here are three steps you can take to begin working through your pain:

Name the Pain

What past or current suffering or struggle is causing your pain? Naming your pain may seem like an obvious step for some. For Ed and me, naming our pain appears simple: we lost a daughter far too soon by earthly standards. But beneath the obvious hurts are many less obvious ones. For example, I'm hurt as a mother—that I couldn't help LeeBeth the way she needed to be helped. I'm hurt as a grandmother—that I won't ever rock LeeBeth's babies to sleep. Like paper cuts on my soul, I'm hurt in a thousand tiny ways, and each of those needs to be acknowledged as they enter my mind as points of pain.

Maybe you aren't sure what's causing you anguish and heartache. Maybe it's an overall disappointment in how your life has gone. Maybe it's something that *didn't* happen. Or maybe you are in pain because of something that happened to someone else. It's critical to spend some time in introspection so that you can identify the source of your pain.

Identify the Potential Impact of Working through Your Pain

Processing your pain will certainly impact you emotionally, but there are other factors to consider as well. For example, there may be financial considerations if you decide to see a professional counselor or enter a treatment program. You may need to take time off work or arrange for additional childcare, which could decrease your income or increase your debt. There may be relational transitions to navigate, such as how family and friends could be impacted.

Know what is required to address your pain so that when you are confronted with a potential obstacle, you aren't deterred from your path. There will likely be developments you can't predict, but acknowledging the "costs" of processing your pain will give you the best chance at continuing the journey.

Identify and Implement Support Structures and Practices

Working through pain requires support from others and personal practices that keep us grounded. We implement support structures and personal practices to answer the question, "What am I doing to work through the pain?" Support structures might include seeing a professional counselor, attending a support group, or consistently leaning into replenishing relationships. Ed and I have never been more thankful for our community than we were when we began walking this difficult journey. We think community is such a crucial resource that we dedicated the entire last chapter of this book to it!

Personal practices might include consistent Bible reading, prayer, journaling, and church attendance and involvement.

LET THE TEARS FALL

Allow us to give you permission to be sad during this process. We encourage you to let the tears fall. Physical acts of grieving, such as shedding tears, are essential for processing pain and grief. Your faith isn't lessened by your tears, and crying doesn't mean you're weak.

Expressing emotion can be hard for all of us at times, but crying is often especially difficult for men. Many men were told as boys, "Be tough and suck it up. Men don't cry." But we disagree, and as it turns out, so does God. Look at this list of men in the Bible—some warriors, kings, and great heroes of the faith—who cried:

Esau (Genesis 27:38)
Jacob (Genesis 29:11)
Joseph (Genesis 42:24)
David (1 Samuel 20:41)
Hezekiah (2 Kings 20:3)
Nehemiah (Nehemiah 1:4)
Mordecai (Esther 4:1)
Brave men (Isaiah 33:7)
Jonah (Jonah 2:2)
Jeremiah (Lamentations 2:11)
Peter (Matthew 26:75)
Paul (Philippians 3:18)

These men are in good company because Jesus also cried (John 11:35). Hey, if weeping isn't beneath the Son of God, the Messiah, the omnipotent, omniscient God, it certainly isn't beneath me.

What do healthy babies do when they come out of the womb? They cry. And to a parent's ears, that cry is a beautiful sound. I remember when each of our children was born, that first cry was such sweet relief. I listened for it and hoped for it because it is a sign of life and health. And it remains a sign of life and health even when we become adults.

Because we are made in the image of God, we can assume that expressing emotions is part of his character and that he gave us the ability to cry for a reason. Crying works out something in us. I'm not a doctor, so I had to google this, but it turns out crying for long periods of time releases feel-good hormones such as oxytocin.[7] You've probably heard of "having a good cry." According to science, that's a thing. Weeping can be good for us.

SHARE YOUR GRIEF AND ANXIETY WITH GOD

Sometimes we aren't sure if it's okay to express our raw emotions to a holy God, or how we should do it even if it is okay. But David gives us this simple instruction: "Trust in God at all times, my people. Tell him all your troubles, for he is our refuge" (Psalm 62:8 GNT). In other words, get it out.

Regularly carve out time to share your pain with God. Get in your car or your closet, or go for a walk. Do whatever you have to do to get alone with God and let it *all* out. Tell God how you feel. God can handle it. "God, I hate every feeling involved with this situation. It's terrible. I'm wiped out." Express that. Pour that out to God.

Then follow the guidance of the apostle Peter: "Cast all your anxiety on him because he cares for you" (1 Peter 5:7 NIV). As we said, anxiety is a kind of baggage. And sometimes to survive a storm at sea, we need to cast our baggage overboard so it doesn't sink us.

I (Lisa) sometimes wake up in the morning with waves of grief crashing upon my heart. I wonder, "Did I do enough to help LeeBeth?" That's when I have to pray and cast my anxiety on the Lord. I wake up and cast my anxiety on him. I eat breakfast and cast my anxiety on him. I ride my exercise bike and cast my anxiety on him. I cast my worries, pain, and cares on the Lord multiple times a day because they keep washing back up on the shores of my heart. My arms are tired from all the casting! I'm sure you've been there too. What do we do? We keep casting.

Because of LeeBeth's salvation, I have great hope. Hope cushions grief and softens the sharp edges as I cast my anxiety on the Lord again and again. So I pray, "God, I'm going to keep giving this to you until it's gone. Until it's healed. Until I have to cast my anxiety only once a day, once a month, or once a year. I know this is stretching me and building my faith. I trust that even this is making me complete because my hope is in you."

ALLOW GOD TO USE YOUR PAIN FOR HIS GLORY

It is often said that time heals all wounds. As I write, today marks the two-year anniversary of LeeBeth going to heaven. In some ways, it seems like a lot of time has passed, and in other ways, it seems like it was just yesterday. Regardless of how little or how much time passes, the pain subsides some on certain days, and other days it burns like a hot flame. But it's false to say time heals all wounds. Only Jesus can fully heal wounds and curb the pain. For me, the more time that passes, the more distance I feel between LeeBeth and me. It was too long ago that I hugged her, talked to her, even worked to get her help. Time has passed, and the wounds are not yet healed.

The more days we walk with Jesus and draw closer to him, the more the pain of our wounds subsides. It isn't because of the time that has passed, but rather the steps taken with Christ as we do the recovery work each day and process the pain with him. The steps we have given you work. They are still working for us and will continue to work over our life's journey as we take it one day at a time, one step at a time, and choose to bring glory to God through our pain.

From the beginning, we knew our journey of grief after LeeBeth's death was a story that needed to be told. It was a messy story and one that no parent, let alone a pastor, would want to share. But we had a choice to make—to hide our pain or to process our pain and, at the appropriate time, share our story for the benefit of others. We chose to place this story, this horrific experience, at the foot of the cross for God to use for his glory.

This is a choice you can make as well. What are you going to do with your pain? However messy your story may be, God can and will use it for his glory, for his eternal purposes, if you are willing to share it.

Ed and I and our children have seen God take our story of suffering, grief, and loss and use it for good in ways we would never have imagined. As difficult as it is to say, after LeeBeth died, her life became a testimony that has changed lives. Our pain has enabled us to connect with others who are vulnerable and hurting. People listen to our words because they know we speak from experience. We definitely don't have it all together, but we trust the only one who holds all things together, and that is Jesus.

How to Redeem Pain

Grow stronger with it.
Give others hope with it.
Glorify God with it.

Pain Today but Not Forever

God gives purpose to our pain. He uses it to develop perseverance in us. He uses it to make us complete and bring us to maturity. He uses it to comfort others. But let's be clear: just because we see the good God is bringing from our pain doesn't mean the pain will disappear. Spiritually speaking, pain has a job to do—to draw us closer to God and to remind us that this earth is not our home.

The apostle James wrote, "Blessed is the one who perseveres under trial because, having stood the test, that person will receive the crown of life that the Lord has promised to those who love him" (James 1:12 NIV).

That is our reward—a crown of life and eternity with

the Lord. On that day, our pain will disappear, and every longing will be fulfilled with God himself. But we don't have to wait on that day to find peace with our pain!

Horatio G. Spafford was born in 1828 and rose in the ranks to become a prominent lawyer and church elder. Spafford had a beautiful house in Chicago, but during the Great Chicago Fire, that home was burned to the ground.

He put his wife and their four children on a ship to Europe. But before the ship could reach the continent, it was struck by another ship. The ship sank. Their four children went overboard, out of the grasp of Mrs. Spafford. When Mrs. Spafford reached shore after her rescue, she sent a telegram to her husband, saying she was "saved alone."

Spafford jumped on the next ship to Europe, and he asked the captain to tell him when the ship passed over the area where his four children had died. When they reached the area, the captain said, "Mr. Spafford, this is it."

Spafford leaned over the rail and wrote the words to the following song:

> When peace like a river attendeth my way,
> When sorrows like sea-billows roll,
> Whatever my lot, thou hast taught me to say,
> It is well, it is well with my soul.
> It is well with my soul.
> It is well, it is well, with my soul.

Horatio didn't write, "Whatever my lot, I feel in my heart . . ." No, God has *taught us* to say it is well. He's given us a reason to have faith and hope. We live in a broken world. But the game isn't over. He sent us his Son, Jesus. He provided a solution to a problem we caused. And though our hearts break again and again, he has taught us to say, "It is well with my soul."

Take a Step

FOUR STEPS ON THE PATH THROUGH PAIN

1. Admit you cannot process pain on your own.

2. Believe Jesus is your loving Lord and anchor.

3. *Choose him daily to lead you by the hand.*

4. Discover hope and healing in community.

- Which of the benefits of pain have you personally experienced? Do you think it's possible to benefit from the pain you're enduring right now? Why or why not?

- Do have support structures and personal practices in place? If not, what steps can you take this week to create some?

- List some things you are learning about yourself and your experience with pain. Name negative emotions that may be taking hold of your attitude toward God and others. Ask God to replace negative feelings and emotions with positive ones.

- How can your pain be used to help others?

CHAPTER 10

One Step at a Time, Together

'Tis so sweet to trust in Jesus! He is my constant companion. Jesus is my salvation, strength, hope, and confidence.

—Lisa's journal, one year
after LeeBeth's passing

I (Ed) was in a fishing tournament outside of Key Largo when it happened. The sun was setting, so my fishing buddy and I were headed back to shore. As we approached the marina, I happened to look out at the horizon and saw something alarming. I punched my friend in the arm.

"Do you see that?" I asked, pointing. "I think that man in the water is in trouble."

We cruised over and, sure enough, the man I had spotted was on the verge of drowning. He'd fallen overboard with his waders on. Waders are tall, heavy rubber boots that are difficult to take on and off. They're usually worn by fishermen, which this guy was. He was also massive—over six feet tall and I'm guessing three hundred pounds.

When waders fill with water, it's nearly impossible to remove them. They become like cement blocks tied to your feet. There was no way this man could have saved himself. My friend and I pulled up next to him in our small boat and grabbed him by the hands. It took all our strength to rescue him, and we ourselves nearly fell in while pulling him into our boat. We took the grateful man back to his boat, and I think all three of us were still in shock as he piloted his vessel off into the distance.

Two things were profoundly true in that encounter. First, that drowning man would not have survived without us. And second, I could never have rescued him by myself. Without my fishing buddy there to help, that man would have died.

It was a vivid reminder that we were never meant to do life alone, and we certainly can't survive and thrive in our storm, struggle, or suffering without help. To make it through seasons of pain and crisis, we need the support of biblical community. Which brings us to the last of the four steps on the path through pain.

Step 4: Discover Hope and Healing in Community

The biblical foundation for step 4 step can be found through-out Scripture, but the apostle Paul says it especially well in his letter to the church at Rome. "Be devoted to one another in love. Honor one another above yourselves. Never be lacking in zeal, but keep your spiritual fervor, serving the Lord. Be joyful in hope, patient in affliction, faithful in prayer. Share with the Lord's people who are in need. Practice hospitality" (Romans 12:10–13 NIV).

Paul's words are a beautiful description of what it looks like to be part of a community characterized by love, honor, service, joy, hope, patience, prayer, hospitality, and more. I'll say it again: we aren't meant to do life alone. That means we aren't meant to do marriage alone, parenting alone, business alone, or faith alone. And we certainly aren't meant to go through trauma or pain alone.

That's not to say there aren't times when we may need to draw away from others for a while. God may invite us to do that. But we need to resist the temptation to stay withdrawn.

When we talk about community, we're not talking about golfing buddies or happy hour sisters. We're talking about people in your life whose relationship with you is built on Jesus Christ. These are people who love, honor, and serve you. They faithfully pray for you and know how to come alongside you because they've been through trials themselves. These are people you can count on when you need help and encouragement.

I sometimes refer to these people as the right "they." I even wrote a book about it titled *Fifty Shades of They.* The right "they" in your life should be:

T—Tough
H—Honest
E—Encouraging
Y—Yielded to God and to your friendship

The body of Christ exists to be your community—your spiritual, emotional, social, and relational foundation. It is your community in which to discover hope and healing, and to help others do the same. One day it will be you showing up in the nick of time to help rescue someone with the hope you've found in Jesus.

Tightropes and Bridges

When I (Ed) have the time, I love to watch documentaries. Recently, I watched *The Flying Wallendas*, about the great tightrope-walking family. In 1970, Karl Wallenda, known as part of the "Great Wallendas," walked a tightrope across Tallulah Gorge in North Georgia. The gorge is almost one thousand feet deep and a quarter mile wide. He walked a tiny cable strung from one side of the gorge to the other. I could see the vegetation swinging around in the background, evidence of the high winds. Watching it gave me heart palpitations. Oh, and did I mention he was sixty-five years old at the time? I'm not sure if he was crazy or brave—probably a little of both! But it was truly remarkable to watch.

At one point, the camera panned across the gorge and I could see a wide footbridge off in the distance that spanned the entire gorge. *Why would anyone choose a tightrope when they could choose a bridge?*

We might ask the same question about our own lives and relationships. Many of us are tightrope walking alone across the hardships of life. But God tells us there's a better option. We can build bridges of strong relationships to help us get from one side of pain to the other.

Us Too

A few years ago, we were invited to speak together at an event, and one of the organizers sent a plane to pick us up. Now, before you start to think we're a big deal, this was a highly unusual experience from start to finish. We weren't on the plane alone either. We were with a dozen or so other people.

On our trip home, we experienced some inconvenience because of an ice storm in Dallas, which was rare. The pilot came over the speaker and said, "It's not looking good, folks." So the pilot kind of played hopscotch and flew to one city and then another to drop off other people. At one stop in the Midwest, a lot of people got off the plane while other people boarded. We didn't know the new passengers, and they didn't know us. They were headed to California, and the plan was to drop us off in Dallas on the way. After twelve hours of hopscotch traveling, we were happy to finally be going home!

As the plane ascended, we introduced ourselves and struck up a conversation with the new passengers. When they found out we were pastors of a church, one of the men mentioned he had seen one of our services online. When he asked what our plans were for the coming year, I (Ed) chose to be transparent and vulnerable.

"I haven't really thought about it much," I said. "I hate to bring up a tough subject, but we lost our oldest daughter earlier this year under tragic circumstances. Right now, we're just taking things day by day."

If you've ever had to give a similar response, you know how awkward it can be. People don't know what to say. But as it turned out, these people were believers. We shared with them the entirety of LeeBeth's story, including her struggle with addiction.

Imagine our surprise when one of the couples began to cry. "We have three daughters too," they shared. "And the youngest has renounced her faith and walked away from the church and from God."

The pain this couple was experiencing was evident. They looked hopeless, on the brink of despair. But as we shared how we were on these parallel tracks—one of joy and one of pain—we could feel the presence of God fill the plane. We explained that we had never believed more in the goodness and sovereignty of God. We were certain God was working for our good, even in LeeBeth's death. When we finished sharing, it seemed as if a few of the emotional weights stacked on their shoulders had been lifted.

Another couple on the plane shared about their son and

daughter-in-law's pregnancy. They had just found out that there was a chromosomal issue with their grandbaby, and it was unlikely the baby would make it to term. They were in pain. We had LeeBeth in our arms for thirty-four precious years. To not have had even thirty-four seconds with her? We grieved with this family.

Our pain, though different, became a bridge between us. We were connected for a precious handful of minutes, ministering to one another through the power of Jesus in and among us. Their pain touched us. It drew us closer to them, closer to each other, and closer to our heavenly Father.

When our plane landed in Dallas, Lisa and I gathered our belongings. "Ed?" one of the passengers said. "Will you pray with us before you leave?" So I prayed over each soul on board, over the fissures in every heart. As we were about to exit, a gentleman who hadn't spoken a word on the flight touched my jacket sleeve.

"Ed and Lisa," he said, "I just have to tell you this: never stop sharing that story."

I believe that was a word to us directly from the throne of God. That's what this book is about. It's not about us. It's not about our church. It's not about how strong we are or even how far we've come. It's about the redemptive and transformative story God is writing with our lives through our pain. It's about being a source of hope for people going through darkness right now. It's about providing support—being the two or three in the boat who are willing to pull someone out of the water and offer them hope and encouragement so that they can live. It's about building bridges to love and support one another.

One of the unforeseen benefits of going through tragic, gut-wrenching, heart-shattering grief is that we have criss-crossed paths with others also walking through pain. It's in moments like the one on the plane that I believe the king-dom of heaven is as close to this earth as it can possibly be. It's like feeling the breath of God on the back of my neck. I feel him all around us, enveloping us with the warmth and peace that come only from him. It's a beautiful kind of strength described by the wisdom writer:

> Two are better off than one, because together they can work more effectively. If one of them falls down, the other can help him up. But if someone is alone and falls, it's just too bad, because there is no one to help him. If it is cold, two can sleep together and stay warm, but how can you keep warm by yourself? Two people can resist an attack that would defeat one person alone. A rope made of three cords is hard to break. (Ecclesiastes 4:9–12 GNT)

We all want that kind of strength, right? But the chal-lenge is that experiencing this type of heaven-on-earth community requires something that makes a lot of us, espe-cially men, uncomfortable. It's called vulnerability.

Vulnerability

One of the reasons we decided to share openly about LeeBeth's death is because we knew our vulnerability would invite others to be vulnerable. That's how it works. Someone has to be the first to lay their emotional cards on the table and say, "This is what I've got." To experience true community, we have to be authentic and transparent.

We wish LeeBeth had been more vulnerable. She didn't lose her life to a physical condition, such as cancer or a car accident; she drank to the point that her body gave out. That's messy. And it's so contrary to what she believed and how she lived most of her life. LeeBeth was a follower of Christ. We dedicated her to the Lord when she was a baby, and she accepted Christ when she was six years old. She worked at our church, and her work ethic was second to none. LeeBeth didn't fit into a box, but she checked off many with her unique talents and gifts.

LeeBeth also had a type-A personality, meaning she was highly motivated to achieve results and could be a perfectionist who expected things to go a certain way. Many times it was like a clock was ticking, and she had a strong opinion of where she should already be in life. That wiring, combined with loneliness, anxiety, and depression—especially after some broken relationships—sent her into a tailspin. She had a therapist. She had us. She had her friends, sisters, and brother. But we can't help but wonder if LeeBeth had anyone with whom she could be completely herself. On the outside, LeeBeth had it all together. But on the inside, there were issues. When we lack vulnerability, it costs us. The price was too high for LeeBeth, just as it is for many others.

I was reading an article this morning about the suicide of a much-loved entertainer. Social media has been flooded with messages of grief and confusion over the loss of someone who was a source of joy and inspiration for so many. Three days before he passed, his wife posted a video of the two of them dancing in front of their Christmas tree, smiling wide.

On the outside, he looked like life couldn't be better—he had a beautiful home, a gorgeous family, a successful career. But obviously, something inside tormented him. I wonder if he had someone with whom he could be vulnerable. I wonder if he had a supportive community he could open up to. His tragic death breaks my heart for his family, friends, and fans. It really does.

Being vulnerable in community may feel like a risk. What if someone judges you? What if someone doesn't accept or like you? But consider the risk of *not* being vulnerable. Consider what's at stake to have no one knowing what you're going through and no one knowing where you're at on the path through pain. Opening up may come with risks, but remaining unknown and unseen is far costlier.

God's Community Center

The kind of community the Bible describes isn't like being a member of the local country club, a player on a sports team, or a member of the parent-teacher association. While it's possible to develop good friendships in those environments, God has more in mind for us. He meant for Christian community to happen in the context of the local church, where we can be inspired by the truth of God's Word and encouraged by others who are pursuing Jesus and living out his grace. He meant for community to be a regular, ongoing part of our lives. The author of Hebrews acknowledged this when he wrote, "Let us think of ways to motivate one another to acts of love and good works. And let us not neglect our meeting together, as some people do, but encourage one another" (Hebrews 10:24–25 NLT).

The Bible refers to the church as the body of Christ. It is made up of many members who each play an important role so that the body is stronger. In his first letter to the church at Corinth, the apostle Paul described the role of community this way: "If one part suffers, every part suffers with it; if one part is honored, every part rejoices with it" (1 Corinthians 12:26 NIV).

The first few days—weeks and months, even—after LeeBeth died are a blur for me (Lisa). But a few moments stand out as particularly meaningful, and they all center on the community Ed and I had built. We had invested in relationships with others who love God, and now that investment was paying dividends. If we wrote about all the meaningful moments when our friends and church family reflected Christ to us and suffered with us, this book would never end. I don't know how anyone could survive a tragedy like ours without a community like ours. And we aren't the only ones who have experienced this kind of love in action.

Let us share part of a letter we received from a man named James in our church a while back.

Recently, my three-month-old daughter had quite a fall. Just prior to boarding an ambulance to Parkland Trauma

Unit, I called a young man I had met in a men's small group at Fellowship Church. He was, in fact, someone with whom I had recently shared some personal prayer requests. I was afraid. This was my only child. Ironically, I did not call one of my employees, a neighbor, or the guy I run with every morning. I called a friend in that men's group who I knew really cared about me. There was an immediate response. Phones began ringing in offices across the metroplex. A prayer chain was started. Men I barely knew were calling the Parkland Trauma Center for updates.

Brooke was diagnosed with a skull fracture. At 11:00 p.m., as I was heading up to the pediatric intensive care, I was paged to the waiting room. There, I was met by an executive with one of the largest consulting practices in Dallas. He had gotten word about our mishap and was standing in the lobby in a sweatsuit with two critical items: a Bible with verses marked for me to read, and a plate of brownies. I hadn't eaten all day. It was so powerful. I walked over to him and embraced him in the middle of that lobby, and I cried on his shoulder. He prayed with me.

Brooke was receiving a CAT scan to determine whether she would need surgery. As we waited throughout the night, I read the verses this friend had found for me, and the promises I found there gave me peace. Brooke ended up not needing surgery. She is completely healed by the grace of God. And I learned what it means to be a part of the church.

Friend, that's a picture of the body of Christ in action. These are the kinds of relationships God calls us to. Not just to receive, but to give. Not just to survive, but to live.

When crisis calls and you need to cry out for help, do you have people in your contacts list you can call or text for help or prayer? Do you have people you know will come through? Are you connected to a body of believers? Have you taken the vulnerable step of giving people who know and love God permission to ask you tough questions? To drag you out of seclusion and walk you into the doors of the church when you're in pain?

The only thing better than having that type of church family is *being* that type of church family. Coming alongside someone in pain completes something in us. It's part of what we're created for. Because two are better than one. Step 4 is to *discover* hope and healing in community. The other side of that is *being* hope and healing in community.

It's true—people have had bad experiences in churches. I bet you or someone you know has a church-related horror story. Ed and I will admit that even our precious church home isn't perfect. Why? Because we're human. And in our humanness, errors and missteps happen.

The church may not be flawless, but Jesus is. And he works through his people in faith communities in ways we wouldn't experience outside of church walls. If you've decided that church just "isn't for you," we urge you to reconsider. You may not feel a deep need for that type of community right now, but one day, there's a very real chance you will.

The Home of Hope and Healing

Melissa's father was an abusive alcoholic who fired shots into their house one night when she was a child. And this is just one example of the extreme dysfunction and abuse she experienced. She lived in fear of what might happen from one moment to the next. As an older teen, Melissa made some unwise choices to get out of her home situation. When her life quickly spiraled into circumstances beyond her control, she found herself wondering, "What next?" That's when a friend invited her to our church. She remembers sitting in the service with tears running down her face, thinking, "Why not give Jesus a chance? I've tried every other way."

In the years that followed, Melissa met her husband at church, and they had three wonderful kids. They built a strong family of their own, and their foundation appeared to be solid. But then Melissa noticed her husband drinking more and more to deal with stress. Given her family history, Melissa was afraid and started questioning God. She had given her life to God, served, tithed, been faithful, done everything right, and now this? She felt like she was right back where she started. But she and her husband had something her parents didn't have—biblical community. They had a church family, a support system, and a foundation built on Jesus.

Her husband worked the Twelve Steps of Alcoholics Anonymous and experienced recovery. Now they both lead support groups to help others. Their kids love the Lord and are thriving. Their marriage isn't perfect, but they have built a home of hope and healing on Christ and his church.

I Can Do All Things

I (Lisa) grew up with a guy named Johnny. I have literally known him all my life. We were in the church nursery together as infants and continued in school together until junior high, when Johnny and his family moved to a neighboring town. Johnny was born with a genetic condition called ectrodactyly, also known as split hand/foot malformation. One of his legs required a prosthetic, one arm was shorter than the other, and both hands were malformed, making even the most basic tasks excruciatingly difficult.

Johnny lived with constant pain, but his resilience was just as constant. He was fearless and full-on, no matter the activity. His parents encouraged him to do anything he wanted to do. Despite his deformed hands, he could hold a bat or a jump rope and keep up with all the rest of us kids on the school playground. Although he had a limp because of his prosthetic leg, it never kept him from competing in whatever sport we were playing that day.

Johnny's family joined the same community pool my family visited to cool off on hot South Carolina summer days. Johnny was a full participant when we played Marco Polo, did cannonballs off the diving board, and swam team races. He just did all of this a little differently. He would sit down, remove his prosthetic leg, and leave it on a lounge chair with his towel. Then he would hop off the chair, climb onto the starting block, and courageously jump into the water when the race began.

Johnny faced psychological challenges as well as physical challenges. He had to deal with the anguish of knowing that his body was so obviously different from others'. That inner pain was part of what drove him to live to the fullest, not missing out on anything everyone else got to do and enjoy. Johnny recently told me that his greatest pain came from his need to prove he could do anything he wanted to do, despite his physical limitations.

Johnny and I have kept up through social media over the years, and our parents remained friends until their deaths. I watched from afar as Johnny pursued a career in the emergency medical field, where he excelled and served others for over twenty-two years. Who better to help someone in trauma and pain than someone who has fought through his own! Johnny also married, and he and his wife, Rhonda, now have two grown children.

When I recently asked Johnny his secret for living such a full life despite his physical challenges, he named several factors, but the most important one was this. In the late eighties, Johnny and Rhonda made the decision to become followers of Christ. They understood that they had been good, churchgoing people, but they didn't have a personal relationship with Jesus. Johnny attributes the healthy and peaceful life he lives now to this decision. He stopped trying to live to prove to others that he could do anything on his own and began to live to prove that he could do anything with Christ alone.

With Jesus leading and guiding you, no matter how hopeless you may feel, how hard it may seem, or how heartbreaking or painful your circumstances may become, keep going. As we partner with Jesus daily, we will truly be able to say, "I can do all things through Christ who strengthens me" (Philippians 4:13 NKJV).

We Are Walking with You

Wherever you are on your journey, know that you aren't walking your path through pain alone. We are walking the same path with you. And we are praying for you.

If you struggle with anxiety, depression, sadness, loneliness, grief, or anything that prevents your joy from shining through, we are praying for you. We pray that God will comfort you, heal you, and give you the wisdom and strength to keep going. We pray that you will have the courage to say, "Pain, you will not stop me!" We pray that, one step at a time, you will move forward. And we pray you will rely on Jesus every step of the way.

Our family verse, which was also the favorite verse of Ed's mother, is this gem from Proverbs.

> Trust in the Lord with all your heart
>> and lean not on your own understanding;
> in all your ways submit to him,
>> and he will make your path straight.
>> (Proverbs 3:5–6 NIV)

We love this promise because it reminds us that the Lord is the one who makes our paths straight. It doesn't say he will make it easy. It doesn't say he will make it smooth. But he will make it straight. And we believe that "straight" leads us directly to him. Through the pain, he will help us to grow stronger and to give him glory by sharing that hope with others. No matter where your path through pain takes you or how long you must walk it, be assured that God is with you every step of the way.

Take a Step

FOUR STEPS ON THE PATH THROUGH PAIN

1. Admit you cannot process pain on your own.

2. Believe Jesus is your loving Lord and anchor.

3. Choose him daily to lead you by the hand.

4. ***Discover hope and healing in community.***

Throughout this book, we have been working the four steps

that can help you navigate the twists and turns of the path through pain. As you continue to work these steps in the days to come, we believe you will experience God in new ways each day, just as we have. Though we have both followed Christ for many decades, we are coming to know him even more intimately as we continue to walk our path through pain with him and as we build bridges of community within our church and with others we have encountered along the way. We pray the same will be true for you.

- Are you prepared to take step 4 on the path through pain? What patterns of thought and behavior would you have to change to take that step?

- What has kept you from being vulnerable in a community? Are you willing to take the risk to become vulnerable for the sake of being known and seen? What's at stake if you stay withdrawn and closed off from community?

- We're sure you can already guess where we're going with this one! If you aren't connected to a faith community, now is the time to connect with one! Not next month. Not next week. *Now.* This week. Look up local churches and visit one. If you're already connected, take that commitment a step further. Get involved in a small group. Volunteer to serve. And when you show up, show up as you—the authentic you. Hold nothing back as you pursue healing through God's holy body.

Epilogue

The last time I (Ed) saw LeeBeth alive, I was tucking her into bed. She was so anxious. Nerves shot. Body worn out. Heart aching. Head spinning.

"I'm going to study a little bit. You just relax," I said. "LeeBeth, I love you."

I kissed her on the forehead and walked into my home office.

I was preparing to give a message on Abraham and Isaac, and I'd just written these words: "And Abraham laid Isaac on the altar."

That's when I heard a sound from LeeBeth's room.

"LeeBeth?"

Silence.

LeeBeth had closed her eyes in hell on earth and opened them in God's glorious heaven. Today, she is healed. She is whole. She is no longer in pain.

See, the ultimate answer for our pain isn't found in a plan, a step, or a process. God's ultimate and resounding response to life's heartbreak is being with Christ in heaven, where there is no more pain and sorrow, no more sin, and no more darkness as we rejoice in his bright and glorious presence. Until then, we will do our best to glorify Jesus as we depend on him daily, taking one step at a time, surrounded and encouraged by other followers of Christ.

People sometimes say, "I'm certain LeeBeth is in heaven, smiling down on all of you." Though we know LeeBeth is in heaven basking in the presence of her Savior—the one she loved, trusted, and lived for—I don't think she has her attention on us. I believe her eyes are fixed on Jesus, and she is worshiping him with the totality of her being. If I were there now, I wouldn't look away for a second.

LeeBeth has completed her path through pain. She is fully healed, restored, and whole.

But what about you? Jesus is not done with you on this side of heaven. He can make you whole and sustain you daily, no matter what you are going through. His purpose is clear. He desires to grow you stronger through your pain, give others hope through your pain, and glorify himself through your pain. We believe in you and have written this book with you in mind, and it has been our prayer while we travel our path through pain that we would be able to encourage someone just like you. You are greatly loved, and what we hoped for LeeBeth while she was alive, we hope for you. The steps work if you work them, and you work them because you are worth it! May God grant you peace as you accept the things you cannot change, courage to change the things you can, and wisdom to know the difference, living one day at a time in complete surrender to Jesus.

Acknowledgments

A book is not just a compilation of chapters, paragraphs, and words. A book is an outpouring of thought, emotion, strategy, and purpose. But these things must be organized in such a way that it all comes together and is beneficial for the reader. As we have written this book, every word has been reflective of our hearts as we have found "a path through pain." Though our words are meaningful, they are often unorganized because of the flow of the heart that pours like a waterfall onto the pages. Oh, how important it is to have intelligent, committed, and loving people to bring rhythm to the words so that the book can be meaningful.

The team that has surrounded us has provided an expertise that has superseded all expectations. We are indebted to each of them in unique ways.

Holly Crawshaw, thank you for listening. You took time to meander through stories and create a plan so that we could articulate the emotions welled up in our hearts. You took our tears that seemed reflective of our weakness and gave them strength in your words, which you adopted as your own. You are magnificent!

A special thank you to Scott Wilson for keeping us on track with great strategic prowess. You spurred us on and were so very caring through it all.

Thank you to Zondervan publishers, who believe that people not only experience pain but also need comfort and assistance in finding a path through it. You have given our pain and grief a voice so that it is worthwhile not only for us but also for our readers.

We express deep appreciation to Esther and Danielle from the Fedd Agency. Your commitment to advocating for the work and guiding us throughout this journey has been remarkable.

Pain and grief affect everyone, and we are so grateful to those who were willing to share, knowing that their stories give strength and hope to others. Chris and Shelly, Tracy and Debbie, Lindsey and JP, Penny and Derric, Kelly and Erica, Melissa and Brad, and finally, to Johnny and Rhonda, thank you for your vulnerability, which has enriched the value of this book and stretched its reach.

To Fellowship Church, the FC team and church members, you will never, ever, ever know what you mean to us. Our family has been on the receiving end of your prayers, your love, and your kind deeds for decades, but what we have felt from you these past several years has touched us to our core.

Most of all, we thank Jesus, our beautiful Savior, who has given us supernatural peace and is our *anchor* every moment of every day!